W9-BQI-007

This

UMI
BOOKS ON DEMAND™

UMI
A Bell & Howell Company

300 North Zeeb Road
P.O. Box 1346
Ann Arbor, Michigan 48106-1346

1-800-521-0600   734-761-4700
http://www.bellhowell.inforlearning.com

Printed in 2000 by xerographic process on acid-free paper

12

Social Studies in the 1980s

A Report of Project SPAN

Irving Morrissett, Editor

Association for Supervision and
Curriculum Development
225 North Washington Street,
Alexandria, Virginia 22314

Project SPAN was supported by the National Science Foundation, Grant No. SED 7718598. Preparation of this volume was supported in part by the National Institute of Education, U.S. Department of Education, under Contract No. 400-78-006, as a part of the work of the ERIC Clearinghouse for Social Studies/Social Science Education. Findings, opinions, conclusions, and recommendations expressed herein do not necessarily reflect the views of the supporting agencies.

Price: $8.75
ASCD Stock No.: 611–82270
ISBN: 0–87120–114–3
Library of Congress Card Catalog No.: 82–72766

Editing:
   Ronald S. Brandt, ASCD Executive Editor
   Nancy Carter Modrak, Managing Editor
Cover Design:
   Al Way, Art Director

Contents

Foreword

OUR SOCIETY'S FAITH IN PROGRESS SERVES WELL MOST OF THE TIME. This confidence motivates extraordinary efforts and brilliant achievements. We assume that progress is directed toward perfection and that perfection is ultimately achieveable. On the other hand, our concept generally acknowledges that perfection is a promise, one never expected to be fulfilled in the present day. We recognize, for example, that the path to perfection may be long, but that we should not loiter as we proceed. As we encounter the frustrations of the journey, we seem to focus increasingly on the problems in our path and recognize less commonly our successes, the distance already traveled, and the problems already overcome. Certainly, under such conditions, we celebrate our successes reluctantly, if at all. We know we should be doing more and achieving more, faster.

This ASCD booklet reflects our notion of progress as it examines contemporary social studies and proposes alternative futures for the field. It merits our attention because of its solid treatment of an area too long honored by benign neglect. It earns our special concern because it reminds us of ourselves, who we want to be as Americans, and how we believe we want to live. It insists that our ceremonial support of the social studies has been empty far too often. And it calls us to realize that our general sense of purpose requires that the social studies be revitalized in our day.

We who know school programs well will recognize the portrayal of social studies in this report. The realities of classrooms are not obscured; they include content emphases, time allotments, pressures on teachers and schools, preparation for teaching, availability and choice of material, the continuing power of the textbook, and the socializing influence of the schools and the social studies in particular. We may wish we did not know all these familiar landmarks and contours; they add up to an impressive sense of the field's stability, even lack of progress. Yet I commend these portrayals because they can help us consider the suggestions for change more appropriately.

Fundamentally, we must know truly, not just recognize, the nature of this field. For one thing, its seeming stability symbolically serves notice that it responds to opportunity, but cannot be jerked into practices that teachers believe are bad. For another, knowing its nature calls for us to know its strengths as well as it flaws, its achievements as well as its missed chances. The social studies has examples of all in abundance. Knowing better and more richly, however, is not sufficient; images of future dimensions of the social studies must be considered.

This report's suggestions constitute one set of images to stimulate our thought and work toward revitalization of the social studies. They are not advanced to be put into practice this year. As we consider them, I hope we will examine their relationships to previous proposals in the field, ponder afresh our basic assumptions and sense of purpose, and invent many possible futures for the social studies.

This task of revitalization, as well as this report, is not for social studies teachers and supervisors alone. It is for all of us. Of course, our colleagues whose specialty is the social studies will find it a special challenge. For the rest of us to believe the tasks are primarily theirs is to deny them encouragement and support and more. It is to deny the schools' and our own specific responsibility to develop for children and youth enriched and increasingly viable social studies. My faith is that all of us are worthy of the present needs and opportunities.

Considering our present perceptions of reality and need and quality in the social studies may be a first step. Thinking and studying and conversing, individually and in groups, will move us along. Our direction is toward revitalization—new life—in the social studies. This general task partakes liberally of our society's concept of progress.

We appreciate the work of Irving Morrissett and his colleagues in summing up the voluminous findings of Project SPAN, and in attempting to focus our efforts toward achieving desired states for the social studies.

Many of the authors' recommendations are directed to the National Council for the Social Studies in particular. Because many ASCD members are also members of NCSS, it is necessary to emphasize that these recommendations are not made with the intent to usurp the interests of NCSS. ASCD has long worked closely with other professional associations of special interest groups within education, and it continues today to support the efforts to those groups who share ASCD's goal of providing quality education for American youth. This booklet is merely one more attempt to make that common goal a reality.

O. L. Davis, Jr.
President, 1982–83
Association for Supervision and
Curriculum Development

Introduction

The Background of Project SPAN

IN THE LATE 1970s THE NATIONAL SCIENCE FOUNDATION, which had long supported curriculum development projects, sponsored three coordinated studies aimed at identifying the current state of social studies/ social science education in the United States. These studies included a series of case studies conducted by the Center for Instructional Research and Curriculum Evaluation at the University of Illinois; a national survey conducted by the Research Triangle Institute; and a survey of literature for the period 1955–1975, conducted by The Ohio State University with the assistance of the Social Science Education Consortium. These studies, using three very different but congruent methodologies,[1] provided a wealth of information about precollege education in natural science, mathematics, and social studies/social science education.

Beginning with those informative studies, SPAN[2] project members set out to describe and assess the current and recent state of social studies/social science education, designate desired states to which social studies might or should aspire, and shape recommendations as to how those desired states might be approached. In addition to the three NSF-sponsored studies, SPAN staff and consultants reviewed hundreds of documents bearing on social studies and, through correspondence and at conferences, sought the advice and comments of many persons throughout the nation.

The basic fact of social studies education at present is that there is a great diversity of opinion from which it is impossible to elicit consensus. There are polar positions on the most basic issues, and a range of opinion between the poles. Some feel that social studies is in need of drastic revision, others that there is little or no need for concern.

The great diversity of opinion about desired states and recommendations that exists in the literature and in the minds of social studies educators throughout the nation was also reflected in the 12 consultants who worked with the SPAN staff throughout the project. Those consultants were chosen for their contributions to social studies literature and

---

[1]A brief description of the studies is presented in the Appendix, page 131.
[2]SPAN = social studies priorities, practices, and needs.

practice and for the range of social studies roles they represented: elementary or secondary teacher, consultant or supervisor at the district or state level, professional association staff member, university teacher.

Given this diversity of opinion, both in the social studies field at large and among the consultants, the SPAN staff (who also held divergent opinions!) must accept ultimate responsibility for the content of the SPAN reports.

SPAN's Report for the 80s

This volume, *Social Studies in the 1980s: A Report of Project SPAN*, was prepared at the request of ASCD. It consists of selected and condensed portions of five reports prepared by SPAN staff members and consultants for submission to the National Science Foundation and distribution to the educational community.

The first section is drawn mostly from the conclusion of an extensive report written by Hazel Whitman Hertzberg as historical background for the project, describing efforts to reform social studies during the period 1880–1980. That report is drawn from a still longer and more exhaustive work now in progress.

The second section focuses on the current state of five critical elements in social studies programming and instruction: rationales, goals, and objectives; curriculum patterns; curriculum materials; teachers; and instructional practices.

The third section, The Future of Social Studies, describes in some detail the six major problems that SPAN staff and consultants believe need to be faced in the 1980s, the "desired states" toward which social studies educators might strive, and recommendations flowing from a comparison of current states and the problems associated with the desired states.

The fourth section describes one of the several major alternatives to the current pattern of social studies considered by the SPAN staff and consultants. It is the work primarily of Douglas Superka and Sharryl Hawke and is the alternative that was developed in the greatest detail. A much more extensive version of the social roles approach, by Superka and Hawke, is also available as a SPAN publication.

Acknowledgments

SSEC Associate Project Director and Staff Associate Douglas Superka and Sharryl Hawke, SSEC Staff Associate, worked with SPAN throughout the project. Bruce Tipple, another SSEC Staff Associate, participated during the early stages of the project as did three SSEC Teacher Associates, Maria Rydstedt, John Zola, and William Cleveland.

Two individuals produced commissioned papers at the request of the project staff. Dana Kurfman reviewed the status of evaluation processes in social studies and made recommendations on needed changes. Hazel Hertzberg wrote an extensive review of social studies reform efforts.

The following consultants also worked with SPAN throughout the project: Lee Anderson, Professor of Political Science, Northwestern University; Mary Vann Eslinger, Social Studies Consultant, North Carolina State Department of Education; John D. Haas, Professor of Education, University of Colorado; Jarrell McCracken, Teacher of Social Studies, Manual High School in Denver; Fred M. Newmann, Professor of Curriculum and Instruction, University of Wisconsin; Elizabeth A. Pellett, Social Studies Consultant, Los Angeles County Schools; Bob Beery, Social Studies Consultant, Rochester (Minnesota) Public Schools; Verna Fancett, Social Studies Teacher Emeritus, Fayetteville, New York; James G. Lengel, Social Studies Consultant, Vermont State Department of Education; John U. Michaelis, Professor Emeritus of Education, University of California at Berkeley; John Patrick, Professor of Education, Indiana University; and Roosevelt Ratliff, Associate Director for Affiliated Units, Association for Supervision and Curriculum Development.

IRVING MORRISSETT
SPAN Project Director and Executive Director
Social Science Education Consortium

Part One
History

Chapter One

Social Studies Reform: The Lessons of History

Hazel Whitman Hertzberg

Reformers' Neglect of School and Classroom Realities

THE DOMINANT REFORM MOVEMENTS OF THE 1960s AND 1970s were strangely oblivious to school and classroom realities, a circumstance that seriously harmed their effectiveness. The reformers assumed they already knew what was going on and tended to underestimate the problems as well as the consequences of change. They were certainly not the first would-be reformers to make such an assumption, but they were unusually insensitive.

The three national efforts that had the most lasting impact on the social studies—the reports of the National Education Association's Committee of Ten (1893),[1] the American Historical Association's Committee of Seven (1899),[2] and the 1916 NEA report[3]—were much more sensitive to realities of the schools and classrooms than were the "new social studies" or the social problems/self-realization social studies movements. The report of the NEA Committee of Ten, which was close enough to current school practice to be practical, articulated the kinds of changes many educators called for. The AHA Committee of Seven began its deliberations with a study of the schools in the United States and western Europe, an investigation that included widespread consultation with teachers. The committee members had a reasonably broad base of information that was buttressed by their own experiences in the schools. The Seven tried to avoid making recommendations that had not already been tested in some schools. The members of the 1916 NEA committee also had extensive experience in the schools and knowledge of developments during the previous quarter-century. They sought modification of the earlier curriculum, not a sharp break with it.

---

[1]National Education Association, *Report of the Committee on Secondary Social Studies* (Washington, D.C.: Government Printing Office, 1893).

[2][American Historical Association], *The Study of History in Schools* (New York: Macmillan, 1899).

[3][National Education Association], *The Social Studies in Secondary Education,* Department of the Interior, Bureau of Education, Bulletin 28 (Washington, D.C.: Government Printing Office, 1916).

All these committees had a far deeper understanding of the continuing socialization function of the schools than had reformers of the 1960s and 70s, and they were broadly concerned with the role of the schools in a democratic society rather than with narrow or highly specialized interests. These were not the only reasons for the success of the earlier reports, but they were essential reasons. The Committees of Ten and Seven and the 1916 NEA committee established a tradition of investigation before recommendation that was followed by many of the other committees of the period.

The AHA Commission on the Social Studies in the 1930s, while sharing a broad perspective with the earlier committees, did not propose a curriculum scope and sequence, and the commission's influence is therefore much more difficult to assess. It is certain, however, that the schools and teachers were unable and unwilling to assume the role the commission advocated. The conflict on this matter seriously divided the commission and constituted the chief criticism of its conclusions and recommendations. This is not to say that the work of the commission was not important or influential. It does suggest, however, that when national reformers lose touch with the schools and classrooms, they limit the impact and the usefulness of their work.

Another example of a reform effort that overlooked the realities of schools and classrooms was the Citizenship Education Project sponsored by Teachers College, Columbia University, in the 1940s and 1950s. The CEP, like the "new social studies" projects, had prestige and support. It was well-financed, used a team/project approach, conducted many teacher workshops, and concentrated on materials production. The CEP proposed to install its version of social studies education in all American schools within a 15-year period, thus sharing with the "new social studies" an inflated conception of its capacity to affect change.

The CEP wanted all schools to extend classroom activities into the community. During the previous half-century, student/community projects had involved comparatively few schools. To induce *all* schools to engage in such activities on a sustained and systematic basis would have required changes in the conduct and organization of schools which were beyond the capacity of a single project, and certainly beyond one that airily brushed aside the difficulties and largely ignored the situation of classroom teachers. Whether such massive change could have been effected at all is a serious question. But it is reasonable to suppose that if the CEP had been willing to concentrate on building a base of support in a relatively few school systems and had not spread itself so thin, it could have, by attempting less, accomplished more.

Reform attitudes towards the inquiry and recitation methods are classic examples of the growing distance between national reform and classroom reality. It is somewhat chastening to consider how frequently various versions of "inquiry" have been advocated during the past century, beginning with the first methods textbook in the 1880s. The

Committee of Ten made some mild suggestions of this sort, and the Committee of Seven further developed advocacy of the inquiry method. Both the Ten and Seven also favored recitation as an alternative to lecture, while staunchly opposing it in its rapid-fire question-and-answer, rote-memorization versions. As in the case of the curriculum, they took care not to go too far beyond classroom practice. Since then most reformers have looked askance at recitation and advocated some version of inquiry.

Despite its low esteem among reformers, the available evidence suggests that recitation has been, and is at present, the typical mode of instruction in the social studies (and in other school subjects as well). The term "recitation" is open to several interpretations, from a mechanical catechism to a more open and free-flowing discussion, but it is always led and structured by the teacher. My own suspicion is that, while recitation has dominated, inquiry has been used in the schools more frequently than is generally admitted. I also suspect that the rapid-fire question-and-answer method is much less common than it was a century ago. There can be little question, however, that social studies instruction has been and is overwhelmingly teacher-dominated—for several reasons.

First, it is an excellent method of mastering factual information. Second, it provides for student participation, which the lecture does not, and most teachers believe in some type of student involvement. Third, it leaves the teacher in control of the classroom and makes clear the roles of students and teacher. Very few teachers do not wish to remain in control of the classroom, whether or not that control is obvious.

The validity of these explanations notwithstanding, the persistence of the recitation in the face of condemnation by reformers and the failure of inquiry to win a commanding place in the classroom in spite of their support deserve serious thought. Does recitation have some positive evolutionary value, as Hoetker and Ahlbrand suggest?[4] Such questions can be answered only by a much more thorough analysis of the classroom itself, both historically and at present. They again point to the need for a closer relationship between national reform and the schools and for reform measures based on a deeper and more comprehensive understanding of schools and classrooms.

The Need for Historical Perspective

The social studies reform movements of the past two decades have been cut off from their own past more than any other major movements in the past century. There are many reasons for this unfortunate case of historical amnesia. One is a pervasive presentism in American society,

---

[4]James E. Hoetker and William Ahlbrand, Jr., "The Persistence of the Recitation," *AERA Journal* 6 (March 1969): 145–167.

greatly accentuated by the intense temporal focus on the present, which is characteristic of television. The rise of the youth culture, characteristically focused on the present, is another. The powerful impact of the social sciences, which tend to be ahistorical, has played an important role. So has the retreat of professional historians from any formal concern with the schools.

Many current issues in social education, as well as other issues yet unrecognized, can be informed and illuminated by our past experience in dealing with them, by knowledge of their historical roots and of the controversies and changes they entailed. The past can never be a perfect or infallible guide to the present, but it can be much more of a guide than we have allowed it to be.

Current retrospectives of social studies education tend to begin with the mid-1950s, when the "new" curricular movements arose. That this time frame corresponds roughly with the adult life span of most of the investigators is probably not coincidental: it is their personally experienced historical reality. But the tendency is unfortunate, because taking that decade as the base line cuts us off from major, critical, and formative parts of our history, when many of the forces now affecting us took shape.

The opportunity to resuscitate the neglected history of the social studies lies before us, and the interest in doing so is growing. Histories of the social studies and of particular components, elements, or factors in their development depend, like all history, on the availability of sources. While for the social studies these sources are by no means complete (and never are), they are both numerous and rich. As new histories are attempted, new sources will be found. The problem is not the lack of sources but their multiplicity. What we need is not a few scattered studies but a vigorous and continuing body of historical writing that will offer a variety of information about and interpretations of our past.

The Need for a Comparative Perspective

We need as well a comparative international perspective on social studies education. The AHA Committee of Seven began its investigation with a study of the teaching of history and allied subjects in European as well as American schools, basing its recommendations on promising European as well as American practices. Perhaps they felt the need for a comparative approach partly because they were attempting to establish history as a school subject. No doubt their choice of approach was also influenced by their own European training and by the then-widespread interest in comparative history. Since that time, relatively few American social studies educators, among them Henry Johnson, have written about the social studies outside the United States. Perhaps the fact that "the social studies" are an American invention has discouraged us from looking elsewhere.

For at least a century, Americans have been attempting an unprecedented task—to bring into the educational system the country's entire youth population. With the exception of a small private sector, this has been an effort under public control, undertaken at public expense. Today the elementary and secondary schools include virtually the entire population of the ages served. Similarly, the number and percentage of people who go on to higher education have increased enormously. The many difficult problems inherent in this experiment in mass education should not be allowed to detract from our recognition of its profound meaning and importance.

All countries shape their schools in markedly idealized versions of their own images and according to their own perceived needs—or the needs that their ruling powers deem essential. The social studies subjects are usually assigned an important role in this task. We should be much more aware than we are that other countries moving toward mass education are experiencing many of the problems that we face today and faced in the past. When we call for a global perspective in other matters, we should likewise apply this perspective to our educational system, especially the social studies. Doing so would enable us to draw on the relevant experiences of other countries as well as give us more confidence in what we ourselves are attempting to do and more pride and commitment in doing it. That we do not see our own educational efforts in a broader international perspective has resulted, I believe, in a preoccupation with our shortcomings, problems, and failures without a balancing consideration of the vastness of our effort and the extent to which it has succeeded.

The Social Studies in the Education of Citizens

Nothing is clearer in the history of social studies reform than the central role assigned to the social studies in the education of citizens. This has been both a mainstay and a source of many of our problems. The social studies cannot take a neutral position on the value and worth of a democratic society, which presents its citizens with the obligation to criticize it as well as to cherish it. Nor can the social studies neglect either the history of this country or the knowledge and skills needed for students to participate effectively in a democratic political order. This is minimally the "knowledge of most worth" central to the social studies. The fact that American history, world or European history, and government/civics have continued to dominate the nation's secondary school social studies curriculum in spite of the indifference or opposition of many reformers and passing fashions and fads is due not simply to inertia, as some have argued, but to a recognition by schools of their centrality in the education of citizens.

The definition of the appropriate education of citizens has been one of the most vexing questions in social studies history. The opposing poles of this definition were early delineated between the Snedden[5] and the Dewey[6] versions of social efficiency. The former envisioned a static, hierarchical society in which everyone had a preordained place. The latter envisioned an open, changing society in which education enabled everyone to find their own places. Dewey's model was the idealized community; Snedden's the juvenile reform school. On the whole, the social studies reformers have been closer to the Dewey pole than to the Snedden pole, but the argument has not ended, nor will it end. The fragmentation of social studies reform has opened the way, probably more than at any time in our history, to some of the contemporary versions of Sneddenism, which tend to be particularistic, vocational, anti-historical, utilitarian, and concerned with procedure at the expense of content.

One aspect of the education of citizens historically has been education about contemporary social problems, their place in the curriculum, and their relationship to history. Some reformers have attempted to base the social studies entirely on social problems, an approach that has not been widely accepted. Typically, we teach history with some reference to present problems, while we teach government or civics with some reference to societal functions. We ensconce some form of Problems of Democracy in the 12th year (although not necessarily under that label) or substitute for it one or more of the social sciences. Neither the "new social studies" nor the personal/social problems social studies have been specifically integrated into the curriculum scope and sequence; how to do so remains unresolved.

The question of advocacy or objectivity in the treatment of controversial issues has been debated time after time by social studies reformers. A few have advocated that the schools and the social studies devote themselves to reconstructing the social order, a position that has been largely rejected by the schools and by most reformers. But reformers have also opposed many of the attempts at censorship of textbooks and other attacks on academic freedom. Historically, the most typical reformer stance on the teaching of controversy has been to teach "both" (occasionally all) sides of an issue in a fair and balanced manner. Today teachers report an extraordinary freedom to deal with controversial issues, although they do not always exercise it.

Student Learning

All the major committees and commissions dealt explicitly with how students learn. Both the Ten and the Seven drew on faculty psychology, albeit a loose version, in their belief in the transfer of learning. New

---

[5]See Walter Drost, *David Snedden and Education for Social Efficiency* (Madison: University of Wisconsin Press, 1967).

[6]John Dewey, *The School and Society* (Chicago: University of Chicago Press, 1899); and *Democracy and Education* (New York: Macmillan, 1916).

theories about learning produced new curricular or methodological emphases. The movement for specific objectives was based on behaviorism. The 1916 NEA committee, basing its ideas on Dewey, asserted that social studies topics should be selected to match the present life interests of pupils or to assist them in their future growth. Many of the citizenship and civics projects involved "learning by doing." Some curricula based on "the needs of adolescents," as in some versions of "core," threw the discipline-based subjects overboard almost entirely. The "new social studies" and the personal/social problems social studies had their own conceptions of student learning, the first largely academic or "cognitive," the second largely affective—problem-oriented, personal, or "cultural."

Despite their many differences, including their brands of psychology, reformers have agreed on two matters. The first is that students learn better when they are actively involved in their own learning. The second is that many students dislike or are indifferent to the social studies subjects. There is substantial evidence supporting both hypotheses.

Why do students seem to like social studies better in elementary school than in secondary school? The current neglect of the social studies in the elementary school does not seem to be due to students. Their dislike of or indifference to the social studies seems to coincide roughly with the onset of adolescence. This is a time when one struggles with and finds a new identity, as Erikson and Piaget contended. It is characterized by some alienation from the past, by ambivalence toward or rejection of history, and by the acquisition of new temporal conceptions as an essential part of an evolving cognitive structure. I suggest that the nature of adolescent growth and change has implications for the teaching of history that have only begun to be explored: the study of history should help adolescents in this fundamental life process. If adolescent students are evolving a new relationship to society as part of a redefinition of themselves, should we not seek to identify ways in which the social studies can help them do it—not in superficial terms of "relevance," but in fundamental ways?[7]

The teaching of "concepts" is a favorite concern of social studies reformers, and "conceptual teaching" is frequently advocated. I have never been able to understand what nonconceptual teaching is, since I think it is impossible to teach the social studies without concepts. Conceptual teaching seems often to mean teaching concepts with content used more or less illustratively. Whether or not one favors "conceptual teaching," it is important to know whether students can

---

[7]See Hazel W. Hertzberg, "Alienation from the Past: Time, Adolescence, and History," paper presented at the Teachers College Conference on History in the Schools, 1977; and "The Teaching of History" in *The Past Before Us: Contemporary Historical Writing in the United States,* ed. Michael Kammen (Ithaca and London: Cornell University Press, 1980), pp. 492–494.

really learn the concepts that are plentifully presented in the social studies.

The scope and sequence of the curriculum itself should be looked at from developmental viewpoints. The fragmentation and incoherence of the social studies presents students with an impossible task: to synthesize and make sense of this jumble at the very time in their lives when they are both resisting and trying to establish new connections and relations with the world about which we teach.

The Social Studies and the Disciplines

The argument over whether the social studies are a federation of subjects or a unitary field has divided reformers since the 1916 NEA report. In practice, federation has prevailed in the schools. The few exceptions are Problems of Democracy courses, some versions of civics, and some of the fused courses, mostly in the junior high school. The first two and many of the latter were also supported by the federationists. "Source study"[8] and the "new social studies" are the clearest examples of federationist attempts to transfer the concerns of university scholars fairly intact to school classrooms. Essentially, these movements involved an argument over the purposes of the social studies. Seen in historical perspective, they were not in the main line of social studies development. Most federationists have argued for the basic citizenship-education purposes of the field while supporting the maintenance of the integrity of the individual subjects. In practice, this usually meant teaching history.

There are good practical reasons for the federationist position. School subjects are derived from organized bodies of knowledge—the disciplines—which comprise cores of information, theory, interpretation, and methodologies that can be adapted for instructional purposes. The unitary-field advocates have no comparable basis on which to build a curriculum. Despite heroic attempts to do so, they have not been able to detach the social studies from their parent disciplines. The example of Harold U. Rugg is instructive. Rugg made a determined, resourceful, and sustained effort to create an integrated curriculum. Discarding the disciplines, he instead based his curriculum on a series of contemporary problems, issues, generalizations, and principles that had been identified by "frontier thinkers." What he ended up with, however, was essentially a history curriculum.

But if the unitarians have had their troubles, the path of the federationists has not been easy. The disciplines themselves change. Over the past century, they have sharpened their differences even while continuing to borrow freely across disciplinary boundaries, and they

---

[8]Studying history using primary sources, a movement in the late 19th and early 20th centuries patterned after the German seminar method.

have also become internally much more fragmented and specialized. These changes have been reflected in the curriculum and in the materials of instruction. In history, for example, the process of specialization overwhelmed balancing efforts at synthesis. The fragmentation of historical research has produced much new knowledge, but its components have not yet been integrated.

The nature of the disciplines and their relationships to each other have constituted one of the most persistent problems in social studies education. One of the contributions of the authors of the "new social studies" was their attempt to delineate the nature of the disciplines, although they made the serious mistake of treating them as eternal rather than changing entities. They did not, however, similarly consider the relationships of the disciplines to each other. The last concerted attempt to examine with genuine sophistication and depth both the disciplines and their mutual relationships was made by the AHA Commission on the Social Studies in the 1930s.

Both the federationists and the unitarians have a common interest in these matters. Because the federationists derive school subjects from the disciplines, they need to examine the disciplines. If all, or most, of the social sciences are to be included in the curriculum, their relationships have to be delineated. Similarly, if the unitarians wish to create a unitary discipline, which will inevitably be drawn largely from the social sciences—and probably from the humanities as well—they also need to examine the natures and the relationships of the disciplines that will contribute to the creation of the field they envision.

Synthesis does not happen automatically. It is much easier to take things apart than to integrate them. Whether or not social studies reformers address themselves to the problem of synthesis, classroom teachers must do so, and it is insufficiently recognized that they are making the attempt with few models and little help. The writers of textbooks have a similar problem. Thus, there are three issues in relation to the disciplines to which social studies reformers should attend: (1) the nature of the several disciplines, (2) the nature of their relationships, and (3) the problem of synthesis, all considered in the context of the value and purposes of social studies education.

The Social Studies and the Learned Societies

Opponents of the disciplines point to the unsuitability of transferring the concerns of scholars virtually intact to the schools, though this has rarely been advocated by reformers—the "new social studies" being a partial exception. The opponents rightly contend that university academics should not be encouraged or permitted to "tell the schools what to do" or to meddle where they have little or no experience, information, or competence. Nevertheless, the social studies need the disciplines.

For many years historians remained close to the schools; they were effective to the extent that they did so and to the extent that they did not focus exclusively on history. Their participation helped to allay or prevent some of the worst abuses of social efficiency in the social studies. This relationship gradually cooled and became increasingly distant after World War II. Some of the social science professional organizations sponsored "new social studies" projects in the main disciplines. Their interest seems subsequently to have faded, along with project funding. Among historians there are a few mildly hopeful signs. A generation of historians has emerged that is deeply interested in teaching. These scholars have produced a literature that matches the social studies reform literature of the 1970s in its exuberance as well as its fragmentation. These teacher/historians, however, have little power in the profession.[9]

The relationship of the social studies to the professional associations of the parent disciplines requires our urgent attention. We need the professional associations as partners, but they are not interested in the partnership. They do not understand the importance of the schools to their own professional health. The most hopeful development may be the growing interest in general education in the colleges, which could provide a basis for cooperation.

Curricular Scope and Sequence

Not since the beginning of the 1920s have social studies reformers attempted to suggest a scope and sequence for the social studies curriculum. The secondary curriculum today is still based fundamentally on the 1916 NEA report. No one really likes it very well, subsequent reformers have generally attacked it, but it endures.

Reformers have been reluctant to suggest an alternative. The usual reason given is that this should be left to the local districts. While I do not doubt the sincerity of these views, it is true that reformers have otherwise felt quite free to urge their ideas and their products on the schools. I suspect that an equally important reason is that no one wants to take on so difficult a task. It's easier to leave it to the schools.

The situation has worsened in several respects in terms of the 1916 NEA pattern. During the past two decades that pattern has been attacked in such a way as to vitiate the sense of purpose, the rationale, for the curriculum itself which the pattern once possessed. The social sciences are now included in the curriculum much more extensively than they have been in the past, and the 1916 pattern cannot accommodate them very well.

Despite the charges that have been leveled against the 1916 report and earlier reports, the curriculum committees did not seek to legislate a curriculum for the schools, nor did they have the power to impose one

---

[9]Hazel W. Hertzberg, "The Teaching of History," pp. 494–504.

by fiat. They made recommendations that were clear, brief, and supported by persuasive rationales. The Ten, the Seven, and the 1916 report all offered some alternative patterns. The many detailed syllabi, courses, and textbooks that were based on the several reports were not included in the reports themselves.

Since every school must have a curriculum scope and sequence and many schools are currently revising their own, it would be useful if some models were developed to aid them. These should be characterized by statements of purpose and by clarity, brevity, and flexibility. One might be based on the 1916 pattern itself, by examining it to see at least how its rationale could be reformulated. But we need alternative models as well. If they are to be genuinely useful to the schools, they cannot depart too far from current school practice. The example of the invention of the Problems of Democracy course and its widespread acceptance, however, shows that it is possible for a "new" idea to evolve as part of a scope and sequence, provided that it corresponds to some important need in the schools.

Teachers today can often persuasively defend a course or unit they are teaching, but they find it very difficult to defend the social studies curriculum as a whole to students, to school boards, to the general public, or to themselves. This is one of the major reasons why the social studies are in trouble in the schools and so vulnerable to attack and erosion.

Dealing with the problem of scope and sequence seems to me much more important than contributing to the proliferation of new curriculum materials. We have a marvelous wealth of such materials already; the problem is to choose among them and to fit them into a coherent curriculum structure.

I do not see any alternative to history and civics/government as the spine of the social studies curriculum. None of the other social studies subjects has the synthesizing and integrating power of history, nor can any of them provide the links with the past that seem to be so desperately needed. It would be folly, however, to ignore the influence and importance of the other social sciences, as some current advocates of a "return to history" seem eager to do. The case for civics/government is self-evident if the historic role of the social studies in the education of citizens is to be maintained and developed.

The 1980s?

The basic lesson to be drawn from a history of social studies reform is the lesson that applies to all history—unless we study it we are doomed to repeat its mistakes. This maxim applies to social studies reform particularly, for two strangely contradictory reasons: first, the enormous wealth of relevant material on past movements and, second, the stubborn refusal of successive waves of reformers, even the historians among them, to come to terms with this history before taking off on "new" reforms. Whatever the reasons for this obtuseness, we can no longer afford it.

At the opening of the 1980s, several trends were curiously like those of the 1950s: concern with "the basics," attention to academically talented students, and demands for more and better mathematics, science, and foreign languages. Should these again coalesce into a movement for curriculum reform, the relationship of the social studies to this development will depend not only on social studies educators' understanding of the past, but also on their ability to assess the new conditions of the 1980s.

The 80s will see deep changes in the human condition, some of them emerging from the past, some of them the result of new scientific, technological, and social phenomena. All of them will affect the social order and the kind of education it provides, including education in the social studies. We cannot predict the state of social studies a decade hence. We can only make informed guesses and express brave hopes based on known conditions to which social studies educators will have to react, actively or passively.

The first and most obvious condition is the aging of the American population, which, based as it is on long-term demographic trends, could be modified or reversed only slowly. The social studies were built on an expanding young population and on the expansion of the schools. We are already seeing the closing of schools on an unprecedented scale. Among the consequences of the present downward or stable demographic trend in the school population will be the necessity of justifying the social studies to an aging taxpaying public. It will also probably mean reduced educational support in general and fewer jobs and less mobility for social studies teachers. However, an aging population is likely to be more historically minded, just because they have themselves experienced historical change. This may mean more support for history.

The second condition is the chronic "stagflation" in the economy, which shows few signs of disappearing in the near future. This will mean less money in school budgets for expensive "innovations" and will probably result in greater reliance on textbooks as the major medium of instruction. Along with creating greater pressures for accountability, economic constraints will force the social studies to fight harder to justify their place in the curriculum.

The third condition is the pervasive influence of television and electronic gadgetry. The influence of TV has received only passing attention from social studies reformers. Few curricula deal analytically or critically with TV: it is simply regarded as another useful audiovisual facility. We know very little about TV's specific impact on social studies learning in the secondary schools, including the models of citizenship behavior that it offers the young. We need to know more, and so do our students. A similar situation obtains with the growing use of computers in instruction.

The fourth and most basic condition is the coming transformation of the United States from an economy based on the expectation of an endless supply of natural resources to one based on the recognition of limited resources, especially energy. This implies a transformation comparable to the industrial revolution. The social studies should not only deal with this historically, they should help students examine how this transformation will change their own values and attitudes and their relationships with society.

All of these trends—and others—are related to our faltering but still living belief in progress and its inevitability. The social studies and their parent disciplines have historically been based on this belief. It has been held by both critics and defenders of the status quo. Reform itself is based on belief in progress, for without confidence in the future and in the possibility of affecting change for the better, reformers would not be in business at all.

Today our belief in inevitable progress is diminishing. People are less confident that their future or their children's future will be better than the present. Nor do they have much confidence in their ability to do anything about it. They are shaken in their once overwhelming faith in the blessings of science and technology. And basic societal institutions—the family and the church, for example—no longer offer assurance of continuity.

Yet the idea of progress cannot be extinguished. Even now it is being reformulated in the light of different expectations about the future. Progress will be seen more in terms of improving the quality of life in a stable society, less in terms of piling up possessions in an ever-expanding economy. Expectations of immediate gains will be modified to accommodate continuing long-term hopes. Such a view of progress is not at all unusual in our history. In any case, the idea itself is so deeply ingrained in the American people that we are much more likely to reformulate what progress means than to give up our belief in it.

If there is any definite, identifiable trend in social studies reform as the 1980s open, it is a search for coherence. This is a reflection of the intense yearning in the larger society for understandable explanations of the perplexities of the 1970s. In the colleges, it is taking the form of an increased interest in general education for citizens as a necessary foundation for both informed civic participation and further specialization. The experiments in a "core" curriculum at Harvard and Stanford are examples. So is the renewed consideration of the introductory survey courses. In the schools, mini-courses have been discarded and districts are reviewing their curricula with a view to greater coherence.

If I am right in my view that the search for coherence is the trend most evident in social studies reform today, we can find much guidance in the past as to how to deal with it productively.

But the past will not be enough. It can guide but it cannot dictate. This is also a lesson of history.

Part Two

The Current State
of Social Studies

Chapter Two

Rationales, Goals, and Objectives

Irving Morrissett
John D. Haas

THERE IS GENERAL AGREEMENT AMONG SOCIAL STUDIES EDUCATORS on the meaning of "goals" and "objectives," but great diversity and confusion about the meaning of "rationale.'

Goals and objectives are understood to mean statements of things to be achieved—usually referring to achievements of students, but also sometimes referring to achievements of teachers or other participants in the educational endeavor. Goals and objectives are sometimes listed without significant ordering or structure; more commonly, they are arranged hierarchically, from the very general to the very specific. While goals are usually understood to mean rather broad aims, objectives refer to narrower or more specific aims. There is no clear dividing line between goals and objectives and the distinction is not always made; the National Assessment of Educational Progress (NAEP), for example, uses the two terms interchangeably.

A goal or objective states *what* you wish to do; a rationale states *why* you want to do it. In education, a rationale should deal with the basic purposes of education; it is sometimes identified with a *philosophy* of education. It must speak to the nature and needs of the individual, to the nature and needs of society, and to the relationship between the individual and society.

This chapter deals first with the subject of rationales, proposing a detailed list of questions that should be answered in constructing a curriculum rationale. There follows a discussion of goals and objectives, focusing mainly but not exclusively on the goals most commonly used in social studies. The final section discusses the uses that are made, and can be made, of statements of rationales, goals, and objectives.

A Suggested Structure for a Curriculum Rationale

The Nature of the Individual

What are the needs, desires, and goals of the individual concerning matters that are physical (or material), social, intellectual, and aesthetic?

16

What are the actual or potential capabilities of the individual for achieving these goals? Capabilities include physical, mental, and moral aspects of potential accomplishment. Stated negatively, what are the physical, mental, and moral limitations on the accomplishment of the individual's goals?

How do the goals and the capabilities of the individual develop over the life span of the individual? What goals are most prominent at various ages or stages of development. What capabilities are present at various ages or stages of development?

How much diversity is there among individuals with respect to goals and capabilities? Is there a large common core of goals and capabilities, or is diversity rather than commonality the outstanding feature of groups of individuals?

The individual and society are closely interrelated. The next element of rationale is the nature of society, which should include an explanation of how the individual and society are related.

The Nature of Society

What is "society"? There are many kinds of societies. Are there some commonalities to all societies? What are the ways in which societies differ?

Is society something apart from the group of individuals that comprise it at a particular time? Does society have a life of its own, more than or different from the lives of the individuals in the society?

What is the individual's relationship to society? Does the individual view society as friendly or hostile, helpful or hindering? To what extent can the individual influence society?

What is society's relationship to the individual? To what extent does it mold or control the individual? How much freedom does society allow the individual in the various domains of life—intellectual, economic, moral, aesthetic, religious, and so forth? To what extent does it influence or set the individual's values and goals?

To what extent does a society maintain its continuity and to what extent is it subject to change? What determines how much its continuity will be maintained and how much it can be changed? What are the processes or means by which society changes? What is the role of individuals and of groups of individuals in influencing continuity and change?

The Nature of Values

How do individuals acquire values? From within themselves? From family, friends, school, religion?

To what extent are values determined by subjective opinions, to what extent by society?

Can some values be demonstrated to have universal validity?

The Nature of Knowledge

Is there an objective reality "out there," such that investigations by and communication among individuals will create a common view of reality? Or is reality a private thing, more or less different for every individual, with each view of reality equally valid?

How do people create or acquire knowledge? What are the processes by which people gather, organize, test, accumulate, and store knowledge?

Are there different kinds of knowledge; or equivalently, is it useful to classify knowledge into various categories? For example, is a classification such as physical science, social science, and humanities useful? Is a classification into knowledge (content), skills, and attitudes useful?

What are the institutional arrangements for acquiring and storing knowledge? Specifically, what is the role of individuals and organizations in forming and perpetuating "subjects" or "disciplines"? What is the role of such subjects or disciplines in acquiring and storing knowledge or inhibiting the discovery of new knowledge?

The Nature of Learning

What characteristics of learners, individually and in groups, are relevant to how students learn?

What motivates students to learn? Is it useful to identify "intrinsic" and "extrinsic" motivations—intrinsic motivations that come from within the individual, such as curiosity or a conviction that the acquisition of certain knowledge might be useful; extrinsic motivation that includes various kinds of rewards and punishments imposed by teachers or others?

Do the system and environment within which learning takes place support the goals of learning?

Are there levels or stages of physical, mental, or emotional development that make certain kinds of learning and methods more suitable at some times than at others? If so, what are these levels or stages, how can they be identified, and how can they be related to particular kinds of learning and methods of learning?

By what processes do students learn? To what extent do they learn by copying the behavior of teachers and other models, by reading, by listening to verbal presentations, by structured or unstructured experiences, by attempting to solve problems that are set for them or which they identify for themselves?

The Nature of the Curriculum

The purpose of all these questions is to provide guidance for selecting goals and objectives and constructing curricula that take account of the essential ingredients of social studies learning—the nature of the individual, of society, of values, of knowledge, and of learning. All of these elements should guide educators in structuring both content and methods. In turn, all that is done in curriculum should be compatible with the rationale on which the curriculum is based.

Figure 1, which illustrates these relationships, indicates that we begin with the individual and society—with their nature, needs, and relationships. We are then led to consider the nature of values and how they interact with the individual and society; thence to knowledge and its relationship to the individual and society; then to how individuals learn and how society is related to the learning of individuals. All of this knowledge of the individual, society, values, knowledge, and learning is then focused on the goals and objectives of a curriculum, with the requirement that they be consistent with the other parts of the system. Goals and objectives should then guide decisions about curriculum content and methods.

The term "rationale" may be used to indicate the basis for selecting goals and objectives, as indicated by the left bracket in Figure 1. Alternatively, the term may be understood to include goals and objectives, in which case it becomes a rationale for curriculum content and methods, as indicated by the right bracket in Figure 1.

Figure 1

Interrelationships of Ingredients in Social Studies Learning

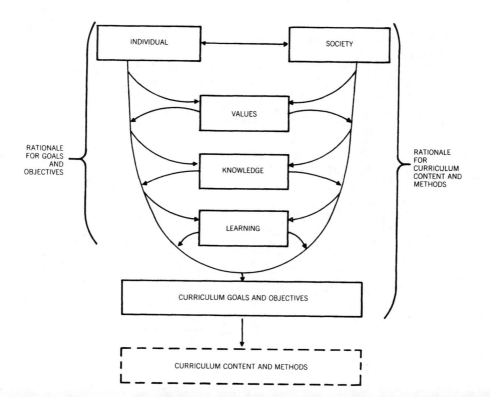

The Scarcity of Rationales

Rationales in the sense just described are virtually nonexistent. A great block to the construction of such rationales is the tremendous amount of effort that would be required; SPAN staff and consultants, in extensive discussions of rationales, agreed that a complete rationale would require a book of many hundreds of pages. Ideally, there should be available to the professional a number of social studies rationales, reflecting different views. Great confusion about the meaning of rationale and a perceived lack of need for them also account for the scarcity of rationales. Jack Fraenkel explains the dearth of rationales as follows:

Courses in educational philosophy are seldom required as part of an educator's professional training. Many social studies methods (or other) professors do not deal with questions of purpose in their courses in curriculum and instruction. Accordingly, rationale-building is something that few people in education have been socialized to do, although arguments to do so have been appearing more frequently as of late (Fraenkel, 1980, p. 93).

Fraenkel goes on to note that "a few fairly well-developed statements of rationale for values education do exist," citing Oliver and Shaver's *Teaching Public Issues in the High School* (1966) and Hunt and Metcalf's *Teaching High School Social Studies* (1968). These volumes give extensive justifications for the curriculum approaches they advocate, as does Newmann, arguing for a curriculum to produce "environmental competence," in *Education for Citizen Action* (1975). But these examples, far above the average curriculum approach with respect to a supporting rationale, still fall far short of the complete rationale model described above.

More frequently than "rationale," the term "philosophy" is used in introducing a social studies guide. This is not inappropriate, since the two terms are closely related. Shaver has noted that "rationale-building is philosophy in its truest sense—the study of ideas and their implications" (Shaver, 1977c, p. 98). The following excerpts are typical of curriculum guides that begin with a statement of "philosophy," as well as of many others that begin with similar statements labeled neither "philosophy" nor "rationale."

We believe that the primary goal of Social Studies education is to prepare students to be active, responsible participants in society, endowed with a healthy respect for the rights of others and rich in the self-confidence that grows out of an understanding of and appreciation for . . . (Sargent and Satterfield, 1978, p. 3).

The purpose of the social studies is to help the individual realize the potential of his autonomy and yet retain sensitivity as an individual who exists in the community . . . (Starritt, n.d., p. 1).

Goals and Objectives

As indicated in Figure 1, goals and objectives should flow from rationales. In this section, the most common goals and objectives in social studies are described. The relationship of these to a statement of rationale or philosophy, if it exists, is usually implied rather than stated.

Citizenship as the Goal of Social Studies

Citizenship or citizenship education, always with the connotation of *good* citizenship, is very frequently cited as the "central," "primary," "overarching," "basic," or "major," goal or "focus" of social studies. A strong concern for citizenship education has been evident from the earliest days of the American republic. Freeman Butts (1980) has reviewed the history of the concerns, debates, and emphases of the advocates of citizenship education in public schools from the 1770s to the present. He demonstrates that there has been a strong and continuing interest in developing civic values and responsible civic action throughout our national history, albeit with considerable diversity as to the meaning of citizenship education. This, he says, is illustrated by the tendency

. . . to vacillate between didactic approaches that ranged between two extremes: those motivated by strong moral, national, or nativist fervor that gave civic education a tone of preachy or pugnacious patriotism; and those that would at all costs avoid political controversy in the schools, and thus turn civic education into pedantic, pallid, platitudinous, or pusilanimous exercises (Butts, 1980, p. 53).

When a single goal for social studies is proposed, it is most frequently citizenship. But whether or not a single goal is proposed, most statements of goals and objectives soon move to some hierarchical or taxonomic structure of goals and objectives. In recent years, these statements have most commonly been headed by a four-part division of goals.

Four-Part Division of Goals

By far the most common general classification of goals, in recent statements, is a division into knowledge, skills, attitudes or values, and participation. "Knowledge" in some form has always been the staple of social studies—mostly factual knowledge—although there has been much controversy about what the content of that knowledge should be. Skills or abilities have a long history as accompaniments to knowledge. Values or attitudes have meant quite different things at different times, varying from unquestioning patriotism and docile classroom behavior to fundamental questioning of personal and social values. Participation is a relative newcomer, also with very different meanings, including both classroom activities and social action outside the classroom.

Knowledge

"The traditional and obvious sources of knowledge for social studies are the social science disciplines" (including history), states the 1979 NCSS Guidelines. According to the 1981 NCSS "Essentials" statement, social studies "focuses on . . . history and culture of our nation and the world, geography, . . . government, . . . economics, . . . social institutions, . . . intergroup and personal relationship, . . . (and) worldwide relationships of all sorts between and among nations, races, cultures, and institutions."

The statement from the California *Framework* is somewhat broader (1981, p. 6):

The traditional and obvious sources of knowledge for social science education are the social disciplines, including anthropology, economics, geography, political science or government, psychology, and sociology. Equally important are the humanistic disciplines. History is foremost among them. Literature, languages, law, ethics, and the arts are also essential components of a balanced curriculum—one that is concerned with knowledge, skills, social participation, and value choices in the social, economic, political, and personal realms.

A question that has occupied some social studies educators is whether the social studies are, following Wesley (1936), "the social sciences simplified for pedagogical purposes," or whether social studies encompass something more than or different from the social sciences. James Shaver (1967) has been a particularly vocal proponent of the latter view and has stated that Wesley's definition "has perhaps done more to stifle creative curriculum work in the social studies than any other factor" (even though Wesley (1937, p. 6) admonished that the "indiscriminate use of 'social sciences' and 'social studies' as synonyms is to be discouraged"). Shaver feels that social studies should be "concerned with the preparation of citizens for participation in a democratic society"—citizens who "can intelligently perceive and reflect upon the critical issues facing the society . . . . Social studies curriculum builders must . . . . draw on sources of concepts other than the social sciences if the intellectual skills taught are to be adequate to the demands of political-ethical controversy" (Shaver, 1967). Excessive reliance on the social sciences for social studies content "leads to inadequate attention to the feeling, humanistic elements of citizenship, and to the needs of ethical decision-making that go beyond scientific empiricism." What is needed is "a shift in emphasis from concern with social science data, generalizations, and reasoning to a concern with values and political-ethical decision-making" (Shaver, 1977b).

Skills

It is difficult to draw a sharp line between knowledge and skills. Defined as "all that has been perceived or grasped by the mind," knowledge swallows up skills and much more. But educators usually make a distinction between knowledge, closely related to memorization, and skills, referring to finding, organizing, and making use of knowledge.

The well-known *Taxonomy of Educational Objectives: Handbook I: Cognitive Domain* presents an extremely useful and well-thought-out distinction between "knowledge," in this narrower sense, and other aspects of cognition:

Knowledge as defined here includes those behaviors and test situations which emphasize the remembering, either by recognition or recall, of ideas, material, or phenomena (Bloom, 1956, p. 62).

Knowledge in the Bloom taxomony does not refer only to knowledge of facts, as it is sometimes interpreted. It also includes knowledge of terminology, methods of inquiry, classification methods, methodology, principles, generalizations, theories, structures, and much more. But it includes only recognition and recall of these elements, not finding, organizing, and using them, which is encompassed in the other five stages of the taxonomy—comprehension, application, analysis, synthesis, and evaluation.

The Bloom taxonomy enjoyed great popularity in the 1960s and into the 1970s, in the heyday of the new social studies, and has unfortunately fallen into disuse in recent years; the Connecticut Guide (1981) makes one of the few current references to the taxonomy. Nevertheless, it has had a lasting impact, in somewhat truncated form. The frequent references to "higher levels" of learning often stem from the distinction made in the Bloom taxonomy between knowledge (recognition and recall) and the uses of knowledge described in the other five levels. Much of what Bloom included in the "cognitive domain" at levels two through six has slipped over into the "skills" category in many listings of objectives.

Values

Values comprise the third common goal of social studies. Some form of values education has always been closely related to social studies. The study of United States history—more so in the past than in the present—has always been associated with instilling patriotic values. Perhaps to a lesser degree, the study of United States government has always been associated with the development of positive attitudes toward our democratic government.

Citizenship education, universally accepted as a part, if not the whole, of social studies, always means *good* citizenship. In addition to being rational and participative, students should be "humane" (NCSS, 1979; California, 1981) and have "positive commitments in thought and action to the democratic values of the liberal political community" (Butts, 1980, p. 118).

Another type of values education, less explicitly proclaimed but more consistently practiced than citizenship education, is the inculcation of values that are conducive to the orderly operation of schools, including respect and consideration for teachers, school authorities, and peers. The prevalence of such inculcation is indicated by the Illinois case studies.

We found a high level of covert moral instruction. It was accomplished partly through ritual, some of which is unique to the school (e.g., testing, reporting attendance, asking permission to leave the room) and some of which is common to the culture (e.g., saying please and thank you, waiting your turn in cafeteria lines).

We considered an act ritualistic if certain aspects of its performance had no direct relationship to the recognized or stated goal of the activity (Stake and Easley, 1978, p. 12:33).

The teaching of values related to citizenship and school behavior is as old as education. More recently, particularly dating from the 1960s and the new social studies, the exploration and teaching of values has broadened substantially. Values are now an explicit part of almost every statement of social studies goals and objectives.

The 1981 NCSS "Essentials" statement lists six "democratic beliefs . . . rooted in the concepts of justice, equality, responsibility, freedom, diversity, and privacy."

In sharp contrast to the lists of values contained in many guides are the various highly structured approaches to values education that have been developed in the last two decades. First among these is *Taxonomy of Educational Objectives. The Classification of Education Goals. Handbook II: Affective Domain* (Krathwohl and others, 1964). This publication, parallel to the Bloom cognitive taxonomy, presents a hierarchy of values—receiving, responding, valuing, organization, and characterization by a value or value complex—which culminates in "the peak of the internalization process" of a set of values (Krathwohl and others, 1964).

Invention and discussion of values education approaches flourished throughout the 1960s and 1970s. Superka (1976) identified and illustrated seven approaches: inculcation, moral development, analysis, clarification, action learning, evocation, and union.

The values education system that has received the most attention in recent years is that of Lawrence Kohlberg. Kohlberg explains that his system is an extension of three levels of moral development postulated by John Dewey and three similar stages of moral development supported by the empirical work of Piaget. Kohlberg (1975) elaborated the three stages into six:

I. Preconventional level
   Stage 1: The punishment-and-obedience orientation.
   Stage 2: The instrumental-relativist orientation.

II. Conventional level
    Stage 3: The interpersonal concordance of "good boy—nice girl" orientation.
    Stage 4: The "law and order' orientation.

III. Postconventional, autonomous, or principled level
    Stage 5: The social-contract, legalistic orientation.
    Stage 6: The universal-ethical-principle orientation.

Despite the heavy intellectual investment made in the various approaches to values education, social studies has not been greatly influenced by these highly structured approaches. There were, however, noticeable effects. Consideration of values became more explicit, exploration of values was legitimized to a certain extent, and a wider range of values found its way into many curriculum guides.

Participation

"Participation" is a relative newcomer to the ranks of knowledge, skills, and values as major goal clusters in social studies. It has long existed in the belief that "learning by doing" is an effective way of learning, and that participation is the duty of a good citizen, but this did not formerly qualify it as a major goal. The addition of participation to the list of major goals can be attributed primarily to the insistence of some leading social studies educators that the traditional commitment of social studies to citizenship be strengthened by more realistic preparation for and practice of active participation in public affairs.

In an article on "Goals for Political and Social Participation," Gerald Marker (1980a) shows that some kind of participation has long been on the agenda of social studies and describes some of the forces that have increased attention to it in recent years. He goes on to state that the rationale for education in citizen participation has been strongly built (by Newmann and others) and that adequate materials for such an educational effort have been developed during the 1970s. The problem now to be faced is one of implementation, and on this he takes a pessimistic view regarding possible progress:

The type of curriculum described by Newmann et al. (1977) requires considerable investment of time and energy on the part of the teacher. Student involvement in the community requires numerous "arrangements" by teachers; community agencies need to be contacted, transportation arranged, evening meetings monitored, etc. It is certainly possible that such efforts "fall of their own weight"; teachers find that they cannot keep up such a pace with the typical five-class day (Marker 1980, pp. 78–79).

"Is it possible," Marker asks, "that our lack of success in this area is partly a function of setting unrealistic goals for ourselves?"

The Neglected Goal: The Joy of Learning

While "joy of learning" might be subsumed under the general goal of values and attitudes, we believe it deserves special attention as an important—and neglected—goal. Under the burden of endless lists of goals and objectives, most of them unattained and possibly unattainable, students and teachers alike may forget that learning can be a joyful experience. Most five- and six-year–olds go to school with a sense of eager anticipation of new learning experiences. The elan lasts through the primary grades, possibly longer, but eventually fades under the burden of routine and bureaucracy. By the time the five-year-olds become teachers, administrators, and curriculum developers, many have forgotten their joyful anticipation of learning—or perhaps they don't dare to mention one more impossible ideal.

Somehow, some critics say, our educational institutions fail to nurture the joy of learning and the natural motivation to learn.

. . . a child is *born* motivated to learn . . . . Learning, in humans, can readily be blocked, impeded, discouraged, or fostered, facilitated, encouraged . . . . But the one thing we don't have to do is motivate. . . . We do not need to urge children to use their brains. Our big task is to get out of their way (Hart, 1975).

Alfred Kuhn, in discussing "self-actualization," refers to

. . . the simple desire to *use* our abilities and faculties. . . . This often means doing for the sake of doing: making for the sake of making, . . . playing for the sake of playing, learning for the sake of learning . . . (Kuhn 1975, p. 67).

Socialization or Social Change?

It has frequently been noted that "socialization" is a major goal of social studies. The term appears in the literature, although not as such in statements of goals and objectives. It is often presented in a negative sense, at least in part—meaning society's efforts to train young people so that they will fit into society and not make trouble—an approach that may include regimentation, indoctrination, and avoidance of educational tasks that stimulate creative, critical, or original thinking.

Socialization is closely related to "Citizenship Transmission," a term popularized by Barr and others (1977), and to "Conservative Cultural Continuity," a concept that has been elaborated by Haas (1979, 1980).

A certain amount of socialization is warranted for every society. A certain degree of orderly behavior, of adherence to behavioral norms, is necessary for the preservation of society. The big question is, to what extent should young people be fitted into existing behavioral patterns?

The Illinois case studies, referring to "socialization as a preemptive aim," show the great concern on the part of teachers and administrators for order in the schools:

Putting it in a nutshell, most teachers seem to treat subject matter knowledge as evidence of, and subject materials as a means to, *socialization* of the individual in school. . . .

The more stern socializers promoted subordination, discipline, a "protestant work ethic," cheerfulness, competitiveness, and heavy investment in getting students "prepared" (Stake and Easley, 1978).

The immediate concern of teachers and administrators, as indicated by this quotation, is for orderly behavior of students in school. This is related to much that has been written about the "hidden curriculum," described as a covert effort, conscious or unconscious, to train students to be docile, unquestioning, obedient participants in both school life and adult life (see especially Fielding, 1981).

Charles Beard pointed to two reasons for tempering socialization with encouragement of critical and creative thought. The first is the need for students to be prepared to meet uncertainties and new situations in the future; the second is society's need to develop leadership (Beard, 1932).

While the schools have placed little stress on preparing students for social change, advocates have continued to press for movement in that direction, mostly with little effect. The history of some of these efforts to the mid-20th century has been well described by Merle Curti (1959), including the efforts of such critics as Henry George, Henry D. Lloyd, Charles Judd, and particularly George Counts and Theodore Brameld. Counts' *Dare the Schools Build a New Social Order?* (1932) is one of the most explicit pleas for the social mission of schools. Brameld, whose writings extended from the early 1930s through the 1960s, was credited by Curti (1959) as "the most vigorous and original exponent of the idea that education could and should improve the social order." Among current writers, Fred Newmann (1975, 1977) stands out as an advocate of educating for social change.

The Multiplicity of New Topics

The scope of social studies has expanded throughout the 20th century—slowly at first, then rapidly in recent years. The expansion took the form first of increasing inclusion of more social sciences and then, in recent years, the inclusion of more special topics and problems. In the late 19th century, the field that was to become social studies consisted mostly of history, much of it ancient and western European history (Hertzberg, 1981). As the concept of "social studies" developed, history became more modern and less parochial, the place of government in the curriculum grew, and over the decades somewhat more attention was given to economics and geography. In the last decade or two, sociology, psychology, and anthropology have made modest intrusions.

Much greater than the growth of the social sciences in the social studies curriculum has been the growth of special topics or problems of social concern. This growth can be attributed in part to our society's increased attention to the problems of war and the environment in the late 60s and early 70s, but even more to the social thrusts of President Johnson's "Great Society," which resulted in funding for many new programs of social action, paralleled by funds to bring these concerns into the schools. For these and other reasons, new programs and materials have been developed for implementation in the schools, many of them falling into the scope of social studies. Included are problems related to minorities, women, international affairs, cities, drugs, law, environment, poverty, aging, consumers, death, values and moral education, and the handicapped.

The increase in the scope of social studies, due to a broadening of the coverage of the social sciences and to the introduction of new topics and problems, has contributed to a multiplicity of goals and objectives. Goals and objectives are often added but seldom dropped.

Uses of Rationales, Goals, and Objectives

A Pessimistic View

Why does social studies education lack a clear, comprehensive, consensus definition and justification? A number of plausible reasons emerge from the data base for this study. One reason may be that parents and teachers see the chief purpose of social studies education as "socialization," by which they mean both the subtle and overt indoctrination of students in the nation's values or ethos and in its norms and mores (Stake and Easley, 1978; Shaver and others, 1979). This suggests that social studies educators should teach that which conveys the nature of American society in order to ensure the social adjustment of the young. Or put another way, teach the young the accumulated cultural heritage of the society to assure cultural continuity. Such a "justification" is by far the most popular (Haas, 1979; Fetsko, 1979; Stake and Easley, 1978).

A second possible reason is that few social studies educators (mainly a few academicians) are concerned about such seemingly esoteric issues. Teachers of social studies in the schools are more concerned with matters of classroom management, instructional materials and strategies, and very immediate objectives than they are with rationales, goals general objectives, or scope and sequence (Shaver and others, 1979a; Stake and Easley, 1978).

A third plausible explanation is that social studies educators tend to be rather autonomous in making educational decisions concerning their field. As such, they make practical eclectic choices in piecing together units and courses, usually borrowing freely from a variety of points of view and resources. Such an approach almost defies justification in terms of a consistent rationale (Wiley, 1977).

The Illinois case studies confirm that social studies teachers have more pressing matters to think about than issues of rationales, goals, and objectives, and other matters that concern social studies theorists, such as scope and sequence and the relationship of social studies to the social sciences.

In a stern address in 1976, James Shaver, then President of NCSS, lectured the social studies profession on "our mindlessness." He quoted Charles Silberman's *Crisis in the Classroom*:

"(W)hat is wrong with elementary and secondary education . . . has less to do with incompetence or indifference or venality than with *mindlessness*."

Silberman goes on to define "mindlessness," by implication, as lack of thought about "purpose, and about the ways in which techniques, content, and organization fulfill or alter purpose" (Shaver, 1977b, pp. 301–02, italics added).

An Optimistic View; or What To Do

A case can be made for viewing social studies as a mindless, disjointed morass, in which the various players are engaged in exercises that are largely unrelated to each other and have a negligible and/or unknown effect on what students learn. But, while there may be truth in that position, it is much too extreme. Many resources are at hand: wisdom old and new that can be mined from a century of critical and creative thought and literature about social studies, and many dedicated people, at all levels of education, who have hope and energy for continued improvement in social studies including, perhaps, the courage to strike out in new directions. In this section we suggest some of the resources and directions that educators should consider as they think about the rationales, goals, and objectives of social studies.

Recognition of realities. The barriers to thoughtful, cooperative, and continuing work on rationales, goals, and objectives as a part of curriculum planning are formidable: everyday duties, community pressures, lack of continuity in planning efforts, organizational and academic jealousies, and much more. A positive approach requires a recognition of these realities, so that the modest progress than can be made will not be subverted by the realities. It also requires that the scarce resources for thinking and planning be used judiciously. The Illinois case studies illustrate one kind of poor usage of resources—setting teachers to work on tasks in which they do not believe; in this case, writing behavioral objectives and constructing accountability procedures (Stake and Easley, 1978). While participation is an important part of curriculum planning efforts, it can be worse than useless if participants lack the required time, interest, or ability.

Communication. Although there may be a regrettable lack of communication and integration among the different acts and actors on the social studies scene, there are many opportunities for communication; and there could be more, with better use of the opportunities that do exist. There is communication within schools in inservice programs, in professional meetings, in many informal contexts, and through journals and books. The participants in these many forms of communication collectively have a great deal of academic learning, experience, folk knowledge, and common sense, all of which could be better mobilized for a continued effort to improve our thinking about rationales, goals, and objectives as means to better curriculum planning and implementation.

Use of history. Many efforts to improve education go forth without sufficient knowledge of previous similar efforts that might be useful. Hazel Hertzberg (1981) has prepared for Project SPAN an overview of social studies reform efforts that goes far toward enlightening us about previous change efforts. Readers can learn much about the work of reformers who could have profited from knowledge of the failures and successes of previous work.

Use of guides to curriculum design. We are not lacking in well-thought guides for designing curricula nor in advice on the place of rationales, goals, and objectives in such designs. Reference to these should be a part of any curriculum improvement effort. Useful contributions to curriculum design have been made by Tyler (1950), Taba (1962), Doll (1970), Davis and Haley (1977), and Pratt (1980).

Work with rationales. Despite the difficulties and seemingly esoteric nature of rationales, they should not be neglected. Much is known that is not being used about the nature of students, society, knowledge, values, and learning. Whether sporadic and piecemeal or integrated and holistic, efforts to improve and use rationales should continue at all levels of social studies education.

Conceptual structures. The concepts and structures of knowledge are sometimes pictured as a fad that came and went with the new social studies. But concepts, structures, generalizations, and theories are the organizational bases for all knowledge—of history, of the social sciences, of social studies, of education itself. They are the basis for both the organization of all knowledge into meaningful patterns and the intelligent selection of those small portions of all knowledge that can be incorporated into a particular curriculum.

Alternative patterns of scope and sequence. The proliferation of new subjects and topics in social studies has brought about a renewed concern for the whole pattern of social studies—its scope and sequence. Although some changes in scope and sequence have occurred over the decades, as described by Wiley (1977) and Gross (1977), the basic pattern has remained much the same since the 1920s (Superka, Hawke, and Morrissett, 1980; Jarolimek, 1981). Much of the current distress with the state of social studies is attributable to the pressures exerted by the process of adding new materials and objectives without removing others to make room. But the problem also stems from the antiquity of the dominant pattern of the social studies curriculum, which probably is not as appropriate for the 1980s as it may have been for the 1920s. Recent calls for a reexamination of scope and sequence include those from Schneider (1980) and Mehlinger (1981), and NCSS has established a committee to consider the problem of scope and sequence. In such an undertaking, it is essential that careful consideration be given to (1) revisions of the current, dominant pattern, (2) an alternative pattern or patterns, including radically different patterns, and (3) the possibility of co-existence of two or more patterns that differ substantially from one another.

This is an extensive and demanding agenda, but one that can be useful in bringing work on rationales, goals, and objectives into a reasonable relationship with educational practice. Perhaps the most important considerations are to keep in view the whole process of educational change, to work for continuity and cumulation in whatever efforts are made, to be realistic, and to take satisfaction in small bits of progress.

Chapter Three

Curriculum Patterns

James G. Lengel
Douglas P. Superka

A MULTIPLICITY OF TOPICS IS TAUGHT under the rubric of social studies. In local and state curriculum guides, National Council of Social Studies position papers, and school course offerings, one can find just about every topic there is. From the three NSF studies alone, one can conclude that social studies curriculum content includes: school, community, home, self, families, neighborhoods, communities, state history, world geography, American history, world cultures, civics, world history, problems of democracy, sex education, home living, intergroup education, driver education, guidance, ethics, philosophy, humanities, student development, free enterprise, communism and totalitarianism, and consumer education.

Even though a convincing argument can be made from this evidence that the social studies curriculum is characterized by extreme diversity, lack of focus, and few if any commonly-held structures, other findings of the studies show a remarkable uniformity in the way social studies topics and course titles are organized on a K-12 basis throughout the nation.

Elementary Social Studies Curriculum

The dominant pattern of curriculum organization for elementary social studies (K-6) is the "expanding environments" framework:

Kindergarten: Self, Home, School, and Community
Grade 1: Families
Grade 2: Neighborhoods
Grade 3: Communities
Grade 4: State History and Geographic Regions
Grade 5: U.S. History
Grade 6: World Cultures (Western or Eastern Hemisphere)

This "expanding environments" pattern is based on the notion that social studies content should begin with the immediate environment of the child (self, home, school) and move outward to the community, state, nation, and beyond. In the past several decades, changes have taken place within this framework. Most curriculum guides and textbooks no longer restrict instruction to a single area. Rather, comparative studies are included so that students have opportunities to go beyond their community, state, and nation to get a view of ways of living in other places in the U.S. and the world. In addition, concepts from the social sciences have been introduced in the primary grades as well as the intermediate grades, thus adding a new dimension to the curriculum (Wiley, 1977). But "topics," usually defined in terms of places, remain the dominant organizers of elementary school social studies curricula.

In the primary grades (K-3), perhaps the most significant current trend is the decreased attention being given to the social studies curriculum. About two-thirds of the K-3 teachers in the RTI survey indicated that inadequate time to teach social studies was a significant problem (Weiss, 1978). Primary teachers in that study also reported that they averaged only 20 minutes per day of social studies instruction compared with 40 minutes for math and 95 minutes for reading (Weiss, 1978). Field observers in the *Case Studies in Science Education* and many district people today report even less time (20 minutes per day, two or three days per week). In many districts science and social studies compete with physical education, art, and music for a daily period. In some schools, the two subjects are not even taught at the primary grades (Stake and Easley, 1978).

Social studies courses in the intermediate grades (4–6) extend the "expanding environments" sequence begun at the primary level to state, nation, and world. But there are several important differences between intermediate and primary social studies. First, in grades 4–6 social studies does not appear to be an endangered species. It still does not receive the amount of attention that reading and math do, but the disparity is less—34 minutes per day for social studies compared with 51 minutes for math and 66 for reading (Weiss, 1978). The decline in social studies textbook sales appears to end around the third or fourth grade and teachers and administrators seem to view social studies especially at the fifth and sixth grades as a stable part of the elementary curriculum. Second, beginning in fourth grade, the topics become more defined so that most students are studying the same geographic regions (Canada, Latin America, and Japan) and certain aspects of U.S. history (exploration, colonial living, and westward expansion). Finally, history and geography receive a much stronger emphasis in these grades than at the primary level.

Secondary Social Studies Curriculum

In 1916 the Committee on Social Studies of the Commission on the Reorganization of Secondary Education recommended generally the following sequence of social studies courses: Grade 7, Geography/European History; Grade 8, American History; Grade 9, Civics; Grade 10, European History; Grade 11, American History; and Grade 12,

Problems of Democracy (social, economic, and political). This secondary pattern might be characterized as two cycles of "contracting environ-ments." The major justification of the Committee for this pattern of organization is revealed in the following quotation from their report:

[T]he course of social studies proposed for the years 7–9 constitutes a cycle to be followed by a similar cycle in the years 10–12, and presumably preceded by another similar cycle in the six elementary grades. This grouping . . . is based chiefly upon the fact that large numbers of children complete their schooling with the sixth grade and another large contingent with the eighth and ninth grades (Dunn, 1916, p. 12).

This two-cycle pattern, then, was conceived at and for a time when few people graduated from high school, when large numbers of immigrants had come to America, when the country was close to entering the first world war, and when historians had a very strong influence on the social studies profession. This pattern is believed to have been fairly common already in 1916. By 1924 one-third of the high schools followed this course structure. It soon became the dominant pattern for secondary social studies curriculum organization in the country (Hertzberg, 1981).

Recent data from the NSF studies and elsewhere indicate that, although some changes in this curriculum pattern have occurred in the last 60 years, and despite tremendous changes in society, the dominant structure of secondary social studies courses today is remarkably similar to that 1916 pattern. Considering in one breath what states require, what students enroll in, what teachers teach, what schools offer, and what state and local guides say, the following pattern of social studies courses (with some reversals in order and some differences) predominates today:

Grade 7: World History/Cultures/Geography
Grade 8: U.S. History
Grade 9: Civics/Government or World Cultures/History
Grade 10: World Cultures/History
Grade 11: U.S. History
Grade 12: American Government and Sociology/Psychology

This pattern reflects several changes from the 1916 scheme. European history has been broadened to world history, which includes the study of the history and culture of Africa, Asia, and other areas. Ninth-grade civics has given some ground to world history, and at the twelfth grade Problems of Democracy has become American government, with many schools also offering social science electives such as sociology and psychology.

There are some exceptions to this typical pattern—variations in the uniformity of these dominant courses. U.S. history courses in the eighth and eleventh grades are clearly the most pervasive courses throughout the country. Since textbooks are used widely to teach these courses and since the most widely used texts are chronological surveys of U.S.

history, the great majority of U.S. history courses are probably survey courses. Wiley (1977), however, notes a trend toward inclusion of more social, economic, and cultural content in these courses. She also observes that "some states and districts have made the junior year course into 'American Studies,' emphasizing certain themes and topics with less focus on chronology" (Wiley, 1977, p. 33).

Elementary-Secondary Articulation

We have just described, analyzed, and discussed the elementary and secondary social studies curricula separately. This reflects fairly accurately how they are treated in the schools, as indicated by the following findings from the NSF studies.
- "The articulation of the social studies curriculum was found to be weak at all grade levels" (Stake and Easley, 1978, p. 13:30).
- Articulation of curriculum across grade levels is seen as a problem by more than one-half of social studies teachers (Weiss, 1978).
- Only one (of 11 sites) had made "some attempt . . . to develop and implement a coherent social studies curriculum in the elementary schools" (Stake and Easley, 1978, p. 13:29).
- In only one (of 11 sites) "did we find indication of a sustained attempt to effect articulation from elementary to junior high school social studies" (Stake and Easley, 1978, p. 13:29).
- "Little concern was expressed by secondary teachers regarding the teaching of social studies in the elementary schools" (Stake and Easley, 1978, p. 13:29).

To be sure, many states and school districts have developed social studies curriculum guides that do outline (at least on paper) plans for K-12 articulation based on either social science concepts, social studies skills, or both. The NSF studies, however, indicate that most teachers ignore these guides. Articulation on paper has not generally led to articulation in the classrooms.

There are many reasons for this lack of articulation between elementary and secondary social studies. One factor certainly is the fact that in most cases they occur in separate schools. This explains why the Illinois case study researchers also observed little articulation between these levels in science and math (Stake and Easley, 1978). This physical and cultural separation of the schools accounts for much of the difficulty in communication. But there are qualitative differences between elementary and secondary social studies that intensify this difficulty.

As indicated earlier, social studies is not considered an important part of the elementary curriculum, especially at the primary level. It is considered and treated as an important part of secondary schools (Stake and Easley, 1978). Moreover, social studies at the two levels is based on different organizational schemes. The "expanding horizons" concept of elementary social studies is based, presumably, on some theory of child development, while the sequence of secondary offerings is based on the "exit points" prevalent in 1916.

The major difference, however, and perhaps the one that determines many of the others, is the difference between those who teach social studies at elementary and secondary levels. Most secondary teachers of social studies teach only that. They are required by the state to be certified as social studies teachers, and to prepare accordingly. Elementary teachers, on the other hand, are predominantly working in "self-contained classrooms" where they teach reading, math, writing, good manners, recess, lunch, nap time, social studies, science, and everything else. And it's often in that order of priority. Elementary teachers teach children; secondary teachers teach history, geography, or government. Their self-perceptions, professional turf, and raisons d'etre can only be very different from one another. Since a common finding of the NSF studies was that the teacher is a primary determinant of social studies education (along with the textbook), it is fair to conclude that these qualitative teacher differences account for much of the elementary-secondary "dis-articulation."

The textbook is another significant factor affecting articulation. Since textbooks are developed separately for the various secondary social studies courses, they tend to reinforce "disarticulation" at that level. At the elementary level, however, the social studies texts usually are developed as part of a series—usually K-6, sometimes K-7, K-8 (Patrick with Hawke, 1982). Frequently, the series are based on some plan for the sequential development of concepts and skills organized within the expanding environments framework. Since this framework has an apparently logical basis for sequential teaching (from immediate to distant settings) and since textbooks are written to fit in within this overall framework, there is probably more real articulation within the elementary social studies curriculum than within the secondary. This level of articulation, however, is probably not as high as in reading and math in the elementary schools.

We are led to one final comment about articulation—both between and within the elementary and secondary curricula. Some educators believe that, unlike math and reading, the content of social studies does not lend itself to sequential development and careful articulation. Some even question the logic of the sequentially-oriented "expanding environments" pattern (see Welton and Mallan, 1976; Joyce and Allman-Brooks, 1979; and Egan, 1978, cited in Schneider, 1980, p. 14). This then could be a final reason for little articulation in social studies—there may be little basis or rationale for it. As this discussion indicates, there is disagreement among social studies educators as to whether or not K-12 curriculum articulation can or should be done. Based on the data analyzed by Project SPAN, however, there can be no disagreement that there is in actual practice little K-12 curriculum articulation in social studies.

Conclusion

The social studies curriculum in elementry and secondary schools today is organized around topics of study (places, continents, events, and subjects) that were established more than 60 years ago. Some changes in the content of that curriculum have occurred. Some variations and exceptions to specific courses at particular grades exist throughout the country. Generally, however, the topics and courses and the order in which they are taught are remarkably similar across the nation. At the elementary level "expanding environments" continues to be the major organizer for social studies. At the secondary level cycles of world history, U.S. history, and government or civics predominate. There is little articulation between elementary and secondary social studies programs. There is little evidence of social studies programs being organized around and actually taught on the basis of other possible themes, such as the social science concepts, social studies skills, student developmental needs, or social issues.

Even though there is no central legal or professional authority dictating the curriculum organization for the schools (as there is in many other countries), the effect is as though there were one. While the dominant elementary and secondary patterns today have their roots in national commissions at the turn of the century, no agency of the federal government has ever mandated them. In the U.S. authority for public education rests with the states. The states issue some curriculum requirements and many suggested recommendations, but few states dictate a complete and binding K-12 scope and sequence. In most states the operation of the schools, including curriculum decisions, rests primarily with the local authorities—school boards, administrators, supervisors, and teachers. Local authorities in over 16,000 school districts with some guidelines and suggestions from 50 different states have managed to establish a pattern of social studies curriculum organization that is extremely similar throughout the country.

This common pattern may be attributed to several factors working together. First, there is tradition. We have had this dominant K-12 pattern for 20 years, 40 years, 60 years, or more. Social studies teachers themselves were "run through" this pattern as students. Parents and administrators also experienced it and expect it to continue. Elements of this pattern have been reinforced in state and local curriculum guides for many years.

Second, few have offered a compelling case for an alternative pattern or patterns. Most of the curriculum projects of the "new social studies" focused on developing a specific new course or working within the existing framework rather than creating a new K-12 curriculum organization. A number of states and districts today have, of course, written K-12 social studies frameworks. Most of these, however, use the dominant pattern even if they also emphasize concepts and skills. Those that propose another pattern may have a difficult time implementing it because appropriate materials are unavailable.

This is the third factor explaining the existence of a nationwide curriculum. Most social studies programs are based on published textbooks. Most textbooks have been written to fit into the dominant pattern in order to ensure a market. It is difficult for an individual teacher, school, or even state to implement, for example, a ninth-grade course in psychology if the only materials available for that age level are civics and world history texts. Likewise, it is difficult to convince a publisher to develop a new psychology text for the ninth grade when most of the country is teaching civics or world history at that level. Paul Goldstein, who has made a critical study of textbook development by publishers, writes, "The surest, least costly way to succeed with new materials is to follow the pattern successfully established by materials already in use" (Patrick with Hawke, 1982). As a result, individual teachers, schools, and districts in different parts of the country and in different geographic settings are confronted with a common nationwide tradition, a set of textbooks that reinforces that tradition throughout the nation, and few if any feasible or better alternatives. Not surprisingly, the principal investigators of the Illinois case studies concluded, the end result is "local acceptance of a nationwide curriculum" (Stake and Easley, 1978).

Chapter Four

Curriculum Materials

John J. Patrick
Sharryl Davis Hawke

CURRICULUM MATERIALS ARE TANGIBLE EDUCATIONAL GOODS that embody day-to-day instructional activities. Various kinds of curriculum materials are used in schools. Printed materials, however, are traditional classroom staples. They include hardback basal textbooks, supplementary books of various kinds, softcover workbooks, study prints, programmed instructional materials, and wall maps and charts.

Significance of Curriculum Materials

Curriculum materials, especially basal textbooks, are the foundation of instruction and learning in most social studies classrooms. The most important curriculum decision that most teachers make is the choice of a textbook. Additional curriculum planning and lesson planning tends to be determined by textbook selection. In the majority of cases, the social studies curriculum comprises the concepts, facts, attitudes, and skills presented in the basal textbook used in a particular course.

Influence of Textbooks on the Curriculum

About 90 percent of classroom time, in both elementary and secondary schools, involves the use of curriculum materials. About two-thirds of this time is spent on printed materials, mainly textbooks (EPIE, 1977).

Current practices seem to be a continuation of past methods of teaching. In 1969, for example, the Texas Governor's Committee on Public Education reported that about 75 percent of students' classroom time and 90 percent of their homework time was spent using textbooks (Wirt and Kirst, 1972). Looking back even further, we find that when the very young National Council for the Social Studies commissioned a survey of selected junior and senior high school social studies programs, the report concluded that "Schools were still 'in bondage' to the textbook with only modest improvements in the use of other instructional materials" (Hertzberg, 1981, p. 38).

In most elementary and secondary schools, textbooks are important bases of curriculum planning, particularly in decisions about the scope and sequence of course content. Observers in the case study research project found that although state education departments and local school districts produce curriculum guides for various courses, teachers tend to disregard them. Instead of such guides, teachers depend on textbooks to guide course organization and day-to-day lesson plans (Stake and Easley, 1978).

A somewhat different view of curriculum influence was found by investigators in a study directed by John Goodlad. Teachers were asked to respond to a question about potential sources of influence on what they teach within a given subject area. Most teachers (over 75 percent), regardless of subject area taught or level or schooling, responded that two sources significantly influence what they teach: "(1) their own background, interests, and experiences, and (2) student interests and abilities" (Klein and others 1979).

It is clear from each of the studies that teachers do not regard state and district curriculum guides to be important influences. The evidence is not as clear cut on the influence of materials, particularly textbooks, on curriculum planning. It appears that teachers, viewing available materials as appropriate for students, do use them in their curriculum planning. However, their choice of particular materials is influenced by their personal backgrounds and the interests and abilities of their students. Having used these personal criteria in selecting materials, teachers apparently feel confident in using the materials to help structure their day-to-day teaching.

Budget cuts in school districts and the high inflation rate must be part of any explanation for teachers' heavy reliance on a single hardback basal textbook. Of all curriculum materials, the basal textbook is the most cost-efficient; it is the best bargain available in the educational products marketplace (Rasmussen, 1979). As one publisher explained, "We are moving away from AV materials because of budget cutbacks" (Schneider and Van Sickle, 1979, p. 465).

From data in the Research Triangle Institute survey, it appears that many teachers are not using (or do not have access to) the most current textbook offerings. Approximately one-third of the elementary teachers used books that were more than seven years old; fewer secondary teachers were using books more than seven years old. However, less than one-fourth of teachers at any grade level had books that were less than three years old (Weiss, 1978). In attempting to distinguish differences in use of current textbooks as related to variables such as region, type of community, size of district, and size of schools, the survey found no large differences and no consistent pattern of differences (Weiss, 1978).

Publishers expect heavy emphasis on printed materials, especially textbooks, to continue. Schneider and Van Sickle concluded, on the basis of a comprehensive survey of major publishers, "The traditional textbook will continue to dominate . . ." (1979, p. 465).

Use of Published Supplementary Materials

Publishers report a continuing and substantial demand for certain kinds of supplementary printed materials. They project a "comparatively steady demand for supplementary books, workbooks, and, increasingly, spirit masters. . . ." (Schneider and Van Sickle, 1979, p. 465). However, publishers emphasize that demand for these supplementary printed materials is slight, compared to the huge market for their hardback basal texts.

In addition to the materials that accompany specific textbooks, various kinds of published supplementary curriculum materials may be used in social studies instruction. The most widely used supplementary materials in elementary and secondary school classrooms are maps, globes, and charts followed by filmstrips and 16mm films (Weiss, 1978). According to a study by the Agency for Instructional Television, approximately 60 percent of secondary teachers use film at least once every two weeks (Fontana, 1980a).

Elementary teachers occasionally use "hands-on" materials, but senior high teachers hardly ever use them. Elementary teachers also are more likely than the secondary school instructors to use photographs, posters, and study prints. Neither the elementary nor secondary student is exposed very much to televised or programmed instruction (Weiss, 1978).

In general, most teachers make slight use of various published supplementary materials. A nationwide study reported that the largest number of respondents said they "neither have used, nor plan to use" supplementary materials (EPIE, 1977, p. 8). Another report suggests that only about a quarter of social studies teachers use a variety of materials to supplement the text (Wiley, 1977).

Locally Developed Materials

Some teachers develop their own materials rather than use published instructional products. When EPIE surveyed teachers, the researchers found that locally developed materials accounted for 30.4 percent of all the materials teachers reported using. Since the EPIE researchers considered it implausible that one-third of all materials would be teacher produced, they elicited a further breakdown from the 11,918 teachers responding to their second survey. In this breakdown they found that 52 percent of the locally developed materials were "worksheets or exercises" and another 27 percent were tests or progress evaluations. In addition, 72 percent of all locally developed materials claimed to be in use were reported by elementary teachers. Secondary teachers developed a higher percentage of tests, but elementary teachers developed a higher percentage of worksheets or exercises (EPIE, 1977).

Teachers report that they lack time to develop their own materials, other than worksheets and tests that stem from textbook content. For example, a case study report of a faculty that attempted to develop materials concluded that, "The packets (teacher-created materials) apparently were created at great personal time-cost to the teachers" (Stake and Easley, 1978, p. 1:52). While these materials were viewed by some as "a new approach to teaching social studies," others saw them as "stuff we have been using for years, but now redesigned into packets" (Stake and Easley, 1978, p. 1:52).

Lack of time, coupled with lack of district financial support for local development and the "comfort" teachers seem to derive from textbooks, has prevented local development from becoming a significant curriculum materials force in social studies instruction. Given the heavy demands on teachers' time, it is not surprising that most of them welcome textbooks, which are, in effect, packaged curricula.

Effect of Materials on Student Learning

A recent study by Mullis (1979) substantiates assumptions about the positive effects of curriculum materials on student learning. Mullis worked with data from a nationally-representative sample of 17-year-olds who were part of the National Assessment of Educational Progress testing program in the spring of 1976. She found that curricular and instructional variables—in particular, the amount of time spent using materials such as textbooks—had a significant effect on student learning of political knowledge and mathematics. The effect was more powerful than the students' type of school or home environment.

Numerous small-scale studies have indicated that the use of specific textbooks and other materials in school can lead to certain knowledge. The materials that have made a difference in student learning were distinguished by clearly-stated objectives and lessons that were connected to the specified ends of instruction (Martorella, 1977). Time on task, as the task is presented through particular materials, makes a difference in student learning.

Reactions of Teachers and Students to Curriculum Materials

What do teachers think of their textbooks? In general, they seem to be satisfied. According to an EPIE survey (1977), 85 percent of teacher respondents believed that their textbooks are "for the most part well suited to most of their students." They believed textbooks facilitate learning. According to another national study, most teachers believe their materials are appropriate for about three-fourths of their students (Klein and others, 1979).

Not only do teachers use instructional materials and feel confident about them, they consider them crucial in instruction. In the RTI study, social studies teachers rated "obtaining information about instructional materials" as one of their top two greatest "unmet needs for assistance"

(Weiss, 1978). The head of social studies at one high school involved in the case study research project stated firmly, "Our teachers do not need staff development. We need better materials . . . ideas (are) good but nuts and bolts help is needed" (Stake and Easley, 1978, p. 13:64).

Many teachers who were interviewed as part of the school case study project expressed strong faith in their textbooks. Teachers made statements such as: "Almost every teacher needs a good set of materials from which to start social studies instruction" (Stake and Easley, 1978, p. 3:33), and "The social studies curriculum at Eastland is a textbook curriculum—because parents want it and the district philosophy supports it" (Stake and Easley, 1978, p. 1:74). The classroom observers who helped conduct the case studies made numerous summary statements such as this one: "Teachers felt surely that all their colleagues could provide first-rate education if you gave them . . . the text and demonstration materials they needed" (Stake and Easley, 1978, p. 5:24–25).

How do students feel about textbooks as compared with other kinds of materials? The only systematically collected data reported on student preference were in the Goodlad study (Wright, 1980). About 70 percent of the elementary students reported that they liked using books, about the same percentage as those who like to use records or tapes, maps and globes, and television. They liked books more than newspapers, worksheets, learning machines, and kits, but not as much as games, films, or filmstrips.

Among middle school students, about 72 percent said they liked textbooks very much or "somewhat," slightly more than said they liked using other books and worksheets. A somewhat smaller percentage of senior high students liked textbooks (68 percent); they had a slightly greater preference for worksheets. Neither middle school nor senior high students liked textbooks as much as other learning modes such as television, games, films, filmstrips, and newspapers.

Textbook Content

During the past 20 years, numerous analytical and evaluative studies of the content of social studies textbooks have been published. In her review, Wiley (1977) found more than 50 such studies. A recent search of ERIC documents, education journals, and dissertation abstracts revealed 35 more such studies completed since 1975.

Following are major general findings about the characteristics of textbooks and how textbooks of today compare to those of 20 years ago.

Connection to Curriculum Patterns

Most social studies textbooks are surveys of particular information linked to curriculum patterns found across the United States. Publishers produce materials that fit the subject matter expectations of this curriculum pattern, thereby aiding significantly in its perpetuation.

Within the current generation of elementary text series, there are some variations on the expanding environments pattern, but they are minor rather than dramatic. For example, some publishers, such as Allyn and Bacon and Houghton Mifflin, focus less exclusively on the neighborhood in second grade and add more content on community, which would formerly have been reserved for the third grade. Fourth grade has long posed a problem for publishers because many states require or encourage state history at this level and, of course, national publishers cannot produce a separate history for each state. Consequently, series published for the last ten years or so have used the fourth-grade text as an introduction to geographic regions of the world. Some of the most recent series, however, have centered fourth-grade study on geographic regions of the United States or on a social history of the U.S. (Scholastic, Ginn, Macmillan). Fifth-grade books have remained quite constant as U.S. history texts, but sixth-grade texts reflect some variety. For example, Rand McNally and Follett offer alternate texts for the sixth grade. Rand's offerings are contemporary world study and world history texts; Follett offers eastern hemisphere and Latin America/Canada texts.

Textbooks are provided as separate entities for grades 7–12. Most focus on a single discipline such as history or geography, rather than taking the interdisciplinary approach used in the elementary texts. Although there is some variety in what is taught in social studies at secondary grade levels in schools across the nation, a major finding of Project SPAN is that there is more consistency than diversity. As a result, at each grade level one or two subject areas tend to dominate textbook offerings from publishers.

Format and Style

Widely used textbooks are alike in format and style. Textbooks in the same subject present similar information and interpretations (EPIE, 1977). Frances FitzGerald noted the basic similarities of high school history textbooks:

Since the public schools across the country now spend less than one percent of their budgets on buying books . . . publishers cannot afford to have more than one or two basic histories on the market at the same time. Consequently, all of them try to compete for the center of the market, designing their books not to please anyone in particular but to be acceptable to as many people as possible (FitzGerald, 1979, p. 46).

The same basic similarities can be found in elementary social studies textbook sets. The differences in these books are more a matter of degree than of radical departures in content, format, or instructional procedures.

A striking change in textbooks is their slick use of graphics and their general attractiveness. Textbooks of today are sophisticated and eye-catching.

Twenty years ago, texts tended to look dreary and forbidding, with print extending from margin to margin, broken only occasionally with "file" photos. Today, textbooks are produced with concern for aesthetic appeal as well as academic value. American texts are probably the most beautiful in the world.

But textbooks tend to be difficulut to read. Perhaps the most common complaint of teachers about textbooks today is readability, which corresponds with their persistent concern that students don't read as well as they should. This concern has plagued textbook publishers, who strive to demonstrate the readability of their books.

Pedagogical Characteristics

Elementary textbooks include lessons in skill development much more frequently than do secondary materials. The most typical skills have to do with reading maps, globes, charts, diagrams, and graphs. Other common skills have to do with critical thinking, decision making, research, communication, and social skills. Nevertheless, textbook content has been largely factual. Most books have not been designed to develop analytic ability. Very little content helps students think critically (Wiley, 1977).

Secondary textbooks include activities that call for more advanced or complex performance of the skills treated in the lower grades. However, there is a relatively greater emphasis in the high school grades on content coverage rather than on skills in dealing with information. Students may be asked to practice various thinking skills, but the authors seem to presume that these skills have been taught in elementary or middle school grades. Thus, high school texts include little direct skill instruction.

There is more diversity in the pedagogy of textbooks. Some textbooks do include lessons that require students to apply information and ideas—to perform systematically at higher cognitive levels. Textbooks of the past tended to foster a "read-recite" style of teaching and learning. They consisted of narrative chapters with end-of-chapter questions to guide recitation. Today's texts often include primary source material and tabular and graphic data in combination with narrative text; civics and government textbooks include case studies. Learning activities are included within and at the end of chapters. These activities are more varied than formerly in style and in the responses they elicit from students (Fetsko, 1979; FitzGerald, 1979; Patrick, 1977).

Treatments of Particular Subjects

Textbooks avoid controversial or sensitive topics. When controversial issues are included, they are usually treated superficially. Social class variations, differences in socioeconomic status, and their consequences, have not been discussed substantially or accurately (Wiley, 1977). Coverage of conflicts between individuals and groups is avoided as well; texts tend to emphasize harmony, social stability, and consensus in their portrayals of society (FitzGerald, 1979). However, today's texts tend to present more accurate information than did texts in the past, and they include greater coverage of issues that were once considered controversial. Also—compared to textbooks in the recent past—they are more likely to discuss society's problems and shortcomings (Fetsko, 1979; FitzGerald, 1979).

Textbooks today depict the rich ethnic and social diversity of the American people. This is a marked change from the texts of the 1950s, which "showed only people who looked like Anglo-Saxon Protestants" (Fitz-Gerald, 1979, p. 82). Numerous studies of textbook content in the 1960s documented the inadequate treatment of ethnic and racial minorities in texts (Kane, 1970; Smith and Patrick, 1967; Remy and Anderson, 1971). Under pressure from minority and women's groups, publishers now pay meticulous attention to the way in which people are portrayed through illustrations and narration.

Textbooks have treated aspects of social science and history content inadequately. Social scientists have criticized texts for *not* presenting their disciplines accurately. A study sponsored by the American Political Science Association expressed strong dissatisfaction with the treatment of political science content in elementary and secondary school textbooks (Remy and Anderson, 1971). In particular, the APSA report castigated typical civics and American government textbooks for failure to reflect up-to-date scholarship in political science.

Studies of economic and geography content in textbooks have also been critical (Wiley, 1977). Criticisms of social science content, or the lack of such content, in elementary textbooks have been especially harsh.

Once again, however, things are better than they were in the past. Present-day textbooks more often include basic social science concepts, generalizations, and descriptions of scientific methods of inquiry than do older textbooks. Social science content is likely to be treated more accurately. Yet most textbooks, including some of those that are the most widely used, still do not provide adequate treatment of social science content.

Effects of Innovative Projects

Textbooks and other curriculum materials developed by federally funded projects during the 1960s and 1970s were designed as alternatives to traditional textbooks. They were meant to be innovative and to lead to significant changes in materials used in schools.

Various studies have documented the limited use of most project materials (Weiss, 1978; Wiley, 1977). For the most part, they were never widely adopted nor have they stood the test of time. Many teachers have reported that project materials based on the inquiry method of teaching have been difficult to use with the majority of students.

However, a study of schools that abandoned new social studies materials after having used them for a period of years suggests that the reasons for abandonment are more complex; for instance, loss of a major advocate, unrealistic expectations on the part of the users, and problems resulting from misapplication (Marker, 1980b). Materials were *not* abandoned because they were no longer seen by teachers and administrators as "new" or because there were too few incentives for continuing to use them.

In contrast to their limited direct impact, some project materials have had significant and extensive indirect effects on publishers and their products. For instance, Wiley (1977) reported that economics and government texts show updated and improved content that reflects current research and standards. Similarly, Fetsko (1979, p. 54) concluded that "the federal government's efforts to improve social studies instruction by influencing textbook publishers to upgrade the quality of their materials has achieved some success."

For the most part, the projects did not develop best-selling curriculum materials. Thus, their direct impact on the school curriculum was slight in most instances, although their indirect effects have been more significant. Some of the improvements in current textbooks seem to have stemmed from the ideas and directives of the various curriculum development projects of the 60s and 70s.

Summary of Textbook Content

In summary, modal social studies textbooks tend to be conventional. The emphasis is on transmitting information about "safe" topics, since noncontroversial textbooks are likely to be acceptable and saleable.

The best of the textbooks can be means to certain important objectives in the social studies, such as acquisition of basic knowledge and skills in using information. Certain other objectives, such as the learning of various attitudes or social skills, can best be met through the use of other educational media and practices.

Textbook Development, Adoption, and Change

The contents of textbooks, and the curricula they influence or dominate, are affected strongly by processes of product development and distribution. Textbook publication is a business that must yield a profit. Thus, the pressures of the marketplace may control substantive decisions of publishers about their products. In addition, the textbook market is constrained by state laws and by various political interest groups who demand a say about what happens in *their* public schools.

Textbook Development and Curriculum Change

There are about 50 publishing companies that produce and sell textbooks to elementary and secondary schools. The top ten companies account for approximately 50 percent of annual product sales.

The cost of developing a new basal textbook for the secondary school is a very big investment. A publisher needs to sell a large number of copies of the new product to break even. It may take two to three years to reach the break-even point, unless the book quickly becomes a best-seller.

Some decisions to launch a textbook development project indicate a publisher's desire to innovate—to meet new needs and trends that market analysis reveals. For example, *Magruder's American Government* was published in 1917 in response to the prescription in 1915 of a brand new twelfth-grade course by a National Educational Association curriculum reform commission.

Usually, however, publishers do not stray far from the tried and true. They know that textbook consumers tend to be very conservative. School administrators and teachers generally have little to gain by making innovative choices—and they may have much to lose if they arouse the wrath of pressure groups who consider themselves guardians of the curriculum.

Textbook development is a careful and conservative process, filled with checkpoints aimed at reducing publisher risk in a very risky business. It often takes anywhere from three to five years to develop a new textbook—from product conceptualization to shiny new book. During this time, market conditions may change. Publishing company executives must be continually alert to new needs and trends and ready to adjust product development plans. Attempts to balance all of the various market forces are likely to lead, more often than not, to "safe" decisions and conservative products.

Textbook Adoption and Curriculum Change

Textbook publishing companies pursue two basic marketing strategies—one for adoption states and the other for "open territories." In adoption states, laws regulate procedures for selecting a list of approved textbooks. The aim is to centralize control over the use of materials in local school systems. In states that are open territories, there are no such regulations. However, local school districts may have their own regulations for adopting textbooks.

There are 23 adoption states, located mainly in the southern and western regions of the country. While the adoption process laws vary from state to state, the core of all the regulations are criteria that set boundaries for selection. Publishers must produce textbooks that, at a minimum, fit the criteria if they want their products to be considered for state adoption.

In 17 of the adoption states, the state government pays for books that local adoption committees select from the approved list. In New York, the state provides a dollar amount per student for text purchase. In six adoption states, the funds are provided wholly or partially from local monies. In the two dual selection states, local districts must choose from a state adoption list if they use state funds, but they can make nonadoption choices if they use local funds. Twenty cities also have regulated adoption processes.

The adoption states account for about 46 percent of the national textbook market (Rasmussen, 1978). Three large adoption states—Texas, Florida, and California—represent 17 percent of that market. Thus, these three states (and to a lesser extent the other adoption states) have a strong influence on the content of books sold throughout the United States (Rasmussen, 1978; Bowler, 1976).

Key target states in the "open territories" are those with the *largest* populations: New York, Pennsylvania, Illinois, Ohio, Michigan, New Jersey, and Massachusetts. Major city districts within open territories include Chicago, Detroit, Philadelphia, Washington, D.C., New York City, Pittsburgh, Minneapolis/St. Paul, and Denver. Marketing strategies in the open territories tend to focus on these big state/big city markets.

Over the past several years, the staff of the Social Science Education Consortium has worked with many school districts in the process of selecting social studies materials. Typically, a committee of six to 12 members, mostly classroom teachers, is appointed especially for the task of selection. At the first meeting the leader gives the committee the ground rules, such as budget figures, deadlines, and special administrative decisions. This person also obtains free sample textbook copies from publishers.

The committee then works in a rather disorganized fashion, with members picking up books, thumbing through them, and asking if other materials are available. At some point the group or the leader may determine some selection criteria to be used in making final selections. The entire process is often completed in two meetings, although some committees meet periodically for several weeks or months before arriving at decisions.

How does the selection process affect the content and design of textbooks? According to Robert Rasmussen, who represents the School Division of the Association of American Publishers:

The diversity of the culture results in a diversity of demands. There are demands for recognition of liberal causes. There are demands for more patriotism or less patriotism and flag-waving. Such causes as the rights of minorities, the rights of women, conservation, improved environment, sex education, family planning, ethnic identity, drug education, consumer education, are only a few of the many causes which come forth in textbook hearings held in various adoption states.

Those who speak on textbook content frequently offer completely opposing points of view. Thus, it is often difficult for the adoption committee to reach a final selection which satisfies all points of view. Ultimately, the criticisms or suggestion(s) reach textbook authors, editors and publishers, and decisions must be made to resist or respond favorably. While it is not possible to satisfy the demands of all people, publishers make a professional effort within the limits of responsible scholarship to deal with potentially controversial topics in a way which establishes some acceptable norm (Rasmussen, 1978, p. 17).

Paul Goldstein, an academician who has made a critical survey of textbook development, provides a somewhat different viewpoint. He says the adoption committees respond to conflicting pressures by selecting "materials that they believe are least likely to offend the holders of any particular view. . . . Schools select, and producers produce, materials that are not likely to upset the delicate balance reached among contending interests" (Goldstein, 1978, p. 4).

Prospects for Change in Curriculum Materials

What does the current state of materials development and adoption mean for the future of textbooks? Primarily it means that radical change in materials is unlikely. Curriculum products that reach today's teachers and students must go through a variety of administrative levels which in turn respond to community input. The system tends to buttress the status quo. Products that tend *not* to incite—that are more bland than spicy—seem to be a reasonable publisher response to the multi-layered road that must be taken to teacher/student users.

Only in local development does the conservatism of the process seem to be short-circuited, since teachers essentially write for themselves in such a procedure. However, the impact of locally-developed materials is generally limited to the district in which they are produced. When good generalizable ideas are generated, local developers have no established dissemination system of their own; nor do they have a normal route to publishers to share their work.

This analysis is not intended as an indictment of the present system or of what it portends for the future. It is merely an explanation of why change in materials tends to be slow and incremental, and why that condition seems likely to continue as long as the current processes of textbook development and adoption are maintained.

Chapter Five

Teachers

Mary Vann Eslinger
Douglas P. Superka

THE TEACHER PLAYS THE CENTRAL role in science, math, and social studies education. The Illinois case studies concluded with perhaps the definitive statement of the importance of the teacher in science education, which included math and social studies:

What science education will be for any one child for any one year is most dependent on what the child's teacher believes, knows, and does—and doesn't believe, doesn't know, and doesn't do. For essentially all of the science learned in school, the teacher is the enabler, the inspiration, and the constraint (Stake and Easley, 1978, p. 19:2).

The centrality of the teacher takes on special significance in social studies. Many school observers noted that social studies teachers appeared to be a particularly diverse lot who have a considerable amount of freedom. At the secondary level, this can result in vastly different ways of teaching the same course (Stake and Easley, 1978). At the elementary level, where the status of social studies is on very shaky ground, the interest and inclination of the individual teacher can determine whether or not social studies is even taught on a regular basis (Stake and Easley, 1978).

Demographic Characteristics

The overwhelming majority of elementary social studies teachers are female, while the vast majority of secondary social studies teachers are male. According to the RTI study, over 95 percent of the primary (K–3) social studies teachers and nearly 80 percent of the intermediate level (4–6) social studies teachers are female. By contrast, 62 percent of the junior high and 75 percent of the senior high school studies teachers are male (Weiss, 1978). Social studies teachers at all levels have had considerable teaching experience; in 1978 they had taught for an average of about 11 years.

In comparison to other secondary teachers, large proportions of social studies teachers described themselves as "liberal" or "strongly liberal" and small proportions classified themselves as "moderate." About the same proportion of social studies teachers and other teachers viewed themselves as "conservative." Elementary social studies teachers tended to be less liberal and more conservative (Wright, 1979). Regardless of their political orientations, the overwhelming impression from the Illinois case studies is that most social studies (and math and science) teachers share the mores and values of their communities (Stake and Easley, 1978).

Academic Preparation

Ninety-five percent of the elementary teachers in the RTI survey felt "adequately qualified" or "very well qualified" to teach reading and math. Only 39 percent considered themselves "very well qualified" to teach social studies. Weiss noted that "elementary teachers' perceptions about their qualifications for teaching the various subjects are consistent with the amount of time that is generally spent in instruction in these areas" (1978, p. 138). Consistent with these findings, Wiley concluded in the Ohio State literature review that "it would appear that elementary teachers were not well prepared in history and the social sciences" (1977, p. 143).

From an examination of numerous studies from the 1950s and 60s and a few after 1970, Wiley (1977) concluded that history still appears to be the dominant area of preparation for social studies teachers. A recent study by the Agency for Instructional Television supports Wiley's judgment. History was the primary area of preparation for about half of the secondary social studies teachers in their survey. Sixteen percent were trained in "general social studies" and the rest were distributed among various social sciences—political science, geography, sociology, psychology, and economics (Fontana, 1980).

While specific information on the nature of this training is not extensive, one can reasonably hypothesize that the university education of secondary social studies teachers has concentrated mainly on the mastery of knowledge within history and the social science disciplines with only superficial attention to the philosophy and methods of teaching these fields to secondary school students (Newmann, 1977; Fraenkel, 1980; Wiley, 1977). At the university, high school teachers have probably encountered one primary model of teaching: the professor passing information *about* a discipline on to students, a model which poorly equipped them in the skills of critical inquiry (Wiley, 1977; Stake and Easley, 1978). They are unlikely to have been exposed to an interdisciplinary course, a synthesis or capstone course, a social issues course or a course giving them practice in the methods of inquiry of the various social sciences (Wiley, 1978).

After observing numerous instances of teachers' failure in handling critical questions in the classroom, the principal investigators of the Illinois case studies suggested:

Most teachers had not had the training that would make them respond "instinctively" to the fruitful observation or the penetrating question of a thoughtful student. They were trained in the same undergraduate courses that *prepare* students in universities for graduate studies. These were seldom research seminars of the sort reserved for doctoral studies—to explore areas of doubt or ignorance (Stake and Easley, 1978, p. 16:8).

The great majority of secondary social studies teachers feel adequately qualified. About 90 percent of the junior high and 80 percent of the senior high social studies teachers in the RTI survey felt that way, as did science teachers at these levels. Sixteen percent of the high school social studies teachers felt "inadequately qualified to teach one or more of their courses," the largest percentage for the three subject areas examined in the RTI survey (Weiss, 1978).

Despite teachers' reports that they felt positive about their qualifications and training in their subject areas, many researchers and commentators have contended for years that the subject-matter preparation of social studies teachers has been inadequate (Wiley, 1977). Usually, however, their criteria for adequacy have not been clarified. Furthermore, little or no relationship has been demonstrated between social studies teachers' subject-matter preparation and their knowledge of the subject or their students' achievements in the subject (Wiley, 1977). Grannis (1970), who reviewed a number of studies over a 30-year period, suggested that "the main function of knowledge of subject matter was to sanction the teacher's role as an authority, a giver of knowledge."

Professional Activities

The most useful source of information for social studies teachers is other teachers, as indicated in Figure 1. Their influence as a source of information about new developments is clear, particularly for primary grade teachers who also value college courses, journals and other professional publications, and local inservice programs. Fewer intermediate and secondary social studies teachers rated other teachers, college courses, and local inservice programs as very useful; but more of them saw journals and other professional publications as very useful sources of information.

Few social studies teachers belong to their national professional organization, the National Council for the Social Studies. The 17,000 members of NCSS comprise only a small portion of the estimated 150,000 to 200,000 teachers of social studies. Even among district supervisors responsible for coordinating social studies, less than 20 percent belong to NCSS (Weiss, 1978). According to the Goodlad study, fewer social studies teachers belong to their professional organization than do teachers of other subject areas (Wright, 1979).

While NCSS may not be a significant reality for most social studies teachers, their professional unions—NEA, AFT, and their local affiliates—are. The professional lives of social studies (and other) teachers are directly affected by these associations in such areas as salaries, release time, contracts, time schedules, and class size.

Social Studies teachers are little aware of or influenced by the results of educational research (Shaver and others, 1979a). This may be because they do not find research useful in resolving the problems with which they must cope on a daily basis (Shaver and others, 1979b). It may be because the findings have not been organized in a way that is efficient for them to study, or that no real attempt has been made to communicate the results to them. It may also be because they see the researcher as "one of those people from the university" who is far distant from the action and who really has no idea of what teaching is all about (Wiley, 1977).

Figure 1
Sources of Information for Teachers

Source	Percentage of teachers rating each source as "very useful"			
	K–3	4–6	7–9	10–12
Other teachers	58%	44%	45%	42%
College courses	46	37	34	34
Journals and other professional publications	39	47	42	45
Local inservice programs	44	38	26	14
Local subject specialists	28	17	22	11
Principals	26	28	19	15
Federally sponsored workshops	16	25	16	13
Meetings of professional organizations	16	13	22	20
Publications and sales representatives	14	10	11	12
State department personnel	2	4	5	5
Teacher union meetings	6	5	7	9

Source: Iris R. Weiss, *National Survey of Science, Mathematics, and Social Studies Education* (Washington, D.C.: National Science Foundation, 1978), p. B-119.

Seventy-three percent of the 7–9 social studies teachers and 42 percent of the 10–12 teachers in the CSSE survey reported that they had attended an inservice course within the three years preceding the Illinois study (Stake and Easley, 1978). Half of the K–3 and 7–9 social studies teachers and over 40 percent of the 4–6 and 10–12 teachers in the RTI survey said they took a college course for credit in the school year when the study was conducted (Weiss, 1978).

The Goodlad results confirm this high level of participation in inservice courses, but also shed some light on teachers' motivations:

At all levels, personal growth motivated comparatively few social studies teachers, and salary increases motivated relatively many of them. Moreover, even though they had attended inservice programs about social sciences, cross-cultural, and cross-national education as consistently as their peers attended programs in other disciplines, the secondary social studies teachers had attended relatively few inservice programs about other professional topics such as curriculum development, teaching methods, classroom management, or child growth (Wright, 1979, pp. 6–7).

Teachers' Views of the Purpose of Social Studies

What do social studies teachers see as the basic purpose and essential nature of social studies? This is a difficult question to answer. First, while university professors spend a good deal of time thinking about these matters, elementary social studies teachers, like their counterparts in other subject areas, do not. Social studies teachers, like others, are more concerned and preoccupied with classroom realities—with making it through the week, month, and year—than with defining their field or clarifying their goals. Few teachers want to focus on the "big idea" of social studies. As one observer noted:

Most teachers questioned about their philosophy of history or historiography had little to say. Their concern was structured by the circumstances of their own classroom. Many seemed content to see to it that students knew the textbook and could discuss current events in the light of the assigned readings (Stake and Easley, 1978, p. 16:12).

According to the Illinois case studies, the "preemptive aim" of social studies teachers (as well as science and math teachers) is socialization:

Each teacher had a different set of purposes, but a most common and vigorously defended purpose was that of socialization. It was intimately related to observance of the mores of the community, submitting personal inclinations to the needs of the community, conforming to the role of the "good student," and getting ready for the next rung on the educational ladder (Stake and Easley, 1978, pp. 16:24).

"Preparation" is an equally important goal of social studies and of education in general. At every level teachers prepare students for the next step. Preparation is, in actuality, merely an extension of the major goal of socialization.

The teachers' views that socialization and work preparation are primary aims of social studies is highly consistent with the views of their communities. Many teachers seemed to share this teacher's conception of the interrelationship:

Teachers are an extension of the parent and as such should teach the value system that is consistent with the community. The community has a vested interest in the schools and has a right to demand that certain values should be taught and certain others not be taught (Stake and Easley, 1978, p. 2:13).

Figure 2 summarizes these findings from the AIT studies on teachers' views of the specific purposes of social studies.

Figure 2
Teachers' Views of the Purpose of the Social Studies

Purpose of the Social Studies	Disagree	Unsure	Agree	N
Teach knowledge of the past	9.6%	37.3%	37.3%	552
Cope with life	2.0	10.5	87.5	550
Think critically	0.4	4.3	95.3	556
Teach knowledge and methods of the social science	14.7	41.7	46.6	554
Promote activity in social and political organizations	15.4	31.2	53.6	555
Prepare for alternative futures	9.4	29.1	61.5	549

Source: Lynn Fontana, *Perspectives on the Social Studies*, Research Report No. 78 (Bloomington, Ind.: Agency for Instructional Television, 1980), p. 8.

Although relatively fewer teachers saw teaching the knowledge and methods of the social sciences as a purpose of social studies, they overwhelmingly agreed that coping with life and thinking critically were. There was much less agreement that teaching knowledge of the past was a purpose. This clearly conflicts with the widespread impression that history is a major aspect of social studies in teachers' minds.

Teachers' Perceptions of Their Problems and Needs

The following factors appear to be the most serious and widespread problems for elementary social studies teachers: belief that this subject is less important than other subjects, insufficient funds for purchasing equipment and supplies, lack of materials for individualizing instruction, out-of-date teaching materials, inadequate student reading abilities, and lack of planning time.

Most elementary teachers indicated the following were not "significant" problems: low enrollments, large class sizes, compliance with federal regulations, lack of teacher interest, teacher preparation, and difficulty in maintaining discipline. More 4–6 than K–3 teachers see "lack of student interest" in social studies as a problem.

The case studies provide ample evidence of the relatively low priority of social studies at the elementary level—in both the schools' and the teachers' value systems (Stake and Easley, 1978). Science shares this low priority and in a few instances it was even lower than social studies in teachers' minds (Stake and Easley, 1978).

Primary teachers appear to accept this low priority and see reading and math as more vital. They may need more time to cover social studies, but not at the expense of these "basics." Overall, social studies at this level is seen as "a low-problem-no-trouble aspect of the curriculum" (Stake and Easley, 1978).

Junior high teachers perceive three major problems: lack of student reading ability, lack of materials to individualize learning, and student apathy. They tended to share these concerns with junior high principals and both elementary and high school social studies teachers (Weiss, 1978). Other problems included large classes, "insufficient funds for purchasing equipment and supplies," and "out-of-date teaching materials." By far the most widespread problem for junior high teachers, however, was the inadequacy of students' reading ability. Over 90 percent of the 7–9 social studies teachers in the RTI survey saw this as "a serious problem" or "somewhat of a problem."

Junior high social studies teachers also rank the lack of materials for individualizing instruction as a serious problem. They are concerned with "what to do with the slow learner." They tend to see the textbook as too difficult even for the average student and impossible for one with low abilities (Stake and Easley, 1978). In addition, they do not have sufficient funds to purchase materials that might help. The problem of reading and materials go hand in hand and cause double frustration for the social studies teacher.

The problem of student apathy or how to motivate students may well be tied to both reading and individualization. How to "spark" students, capture their interest, and at the same time hold their respect are major hurdles (Stake and Easley, 1978).

Senior high school social studies teachers' perceived problems and needs were similar to those of their junior high counterparts. Their top three problems were "inadequate student reading abilities," "lack of student interest in the subject," and "lack of materials for individualizing instruction." Evidence from the case studies reinforced these findings (Stake and Easley, 1978). Other problems that seem to be fairly widespread, though not as serious, include inadequate facilities, lack of funds, out-of-date materials, and large class sizes.

Three problems appear to be more widespread at the high school level than at the junior high level. Nearly two-thirds of the senior high social studies teachers saw "inadequate articulation across grade levels" as a serious problem, while only 50 percent viewed this as a problem at the junior high level. More high school teachers also perceived lack of planning time to be a problem than did junior high teachers. Finally, while most junior high social studies teachers felt that lack of importance of their subject was no significant problem, most high school teachers did. Fewer high school science teachers and considerably fewer math teachers regarded this as a problem, despite the fact that social studies requirements at the high school level are still among the most stringent.

Teachers' Level of Satisfaction

Popular magazines have recently published articles about teachers' problems in schools and why "good" teachers are leaving the profession. The most extensive treatment was a cover story in *Time* on June 16, 1980, entitled "Help! Teacher Can't Teach!"

Teachers leaving the profession cite the lack of student motivation and interest as a major frustration (Walker, 1978). So did the teachers in the NSF studies, one claiming that students' lack of motivation was so great a problem that she felt she had to justify her right to teach (Stake and Easley, 1978). Other teachers claimed that students sought out classes requiring a minimum amount of work and insisted that getting a good grade in order to be admitted to college was a primary motivating factor for students (Stake and Easley, 1978). In general, more secondary than elementary teachers cite motivation as a problem (Stake and Easley, 1978).

"Teacher burnout" is a current term and concern—and an oft-cited reason for teacher frustration. The myriad demands placed on teachers add to their frustration:

Teachers are at times expected to be surrogate parents, grandparents, siblings, priests, therapists, wardens, biographers, babysitters, and friends. They are intermediaries for the school [in which they are] expected to feed the hungry, restore the deprived, redirect the alienated, energize the lethargic, and calm the hyperactive, as well, of course, as educate the ignorant, train the naive, and inspire the downhearted. Many enjoy the challenge. Others are frustrated (Stake and Easley, 1978, pp. B-15–16).

This frustration is diffused, not focusing on any one aspect of the school day. For some, the frustration results from the restricted life of teachers in schools:

Some teachers leave the system because they begin to get a boxed-in feeling. They don't like knowing that every day at the same time, they will be in a classroom, locked in for 50 minutes until the changing bell rings, with no time for a cup of coffee, to go to the bathroom or just to shake the cobwebs out of their heads (Walker, 1978, p. 144).

It is difficult to determine from the case studies how widespread dissatisfaction is among social studies teachers. The individual case studies contain some examples of social studies teachers who express considerable satisfaction with their jobs (Stake and Easley, 1978). They also contain, however, numerous examples of staleness, frustration, and dissatisfaction even among the "star" teachers (Stake and Easley, 1978). There were also clear indications that elementary teachers were more satisfied than secondary teachers (Stake and Easley, 1978).

While teacher burnout and professional dissatisfaction exist throughout the profession, there is some evidence in the Goodlad study that these feelings are more widespread among social studies teachers, especially at the secondary levels. Social studies teachers' "initial career expectations had been fulfilled less consistently than were those of other teachers" (Wright, 1979, p. 4). This was most prevalent at the middle school level.

Freedom and Diversity

Elementary and secondary teachers are remarkably free to do what they want in their classrooms, although some forces work to restrict that freedom or to standardize instruction, such as the textbook and curriculum guides. But teachers retain considerable autonomy, largely because they work alone. The principal investigators of the Illinois case studies make a strong point about this aspect of teachers' professional lives:

We found the teacher working alone. During most of the day the classroom was filled with youngsters. Many helped the teacher, often the talk was person-to-person. Sometimes an aide was there, or a parent, or a cadet teacher. Other teachers influenced what the teacher did, but the teacher worked very much alone. Even those few teachers who were "team teaching" were trading-off rather than sharing teaching responsibility. The teacher was little dependent on any other adult, and the dependence of other professional educators on her or him was more rhetorical than apparent. It would be unrealistic to say that the teachers we saw were subordinate to a head of a department or administrator or part of an instructional team. They worked alone (Stake and Easley, 1978, p. 16:27).

What goes on inside the four walls of the classroom is pretty much up to teachers. For most, the classroom is "personal space." Here they have considerable freedom to be themselves, to teach in the manner they deem best for learning, and to decide what ought to be learned. They recognize and act upon the belief that this condition will hold as long as they do not cross the stated or unstated lines drawn by the administration, the board of education, or the community. "Personal space" also exists to the extent they are able to command cooperative student behavior and respect for their authority.

The second quality—diversity—seems particularly characteristic of social studies teachers. Many of the case study observers noted the tremendous diversity found in teachers at both the elementary and secondary levels. While there were some references generally to idiosyncratic teaching styles, several observers commented specifically that there was more diversity and variation among socal studies teachers than among math and science teachers (Stake and Easley, 1978). This diversity was reflected in their views of the big ideas of social studies, how they taught social studies, and what they taught (Stake and Easley, 1978). It was also reflected in how often teachers, parents, administrators, and students talked about "strong" teachers and "weak" teachers, or ordinary teachers and "glow" teachers.

Conclusion

Research has confirmed what many people involved in schools have known for a long time: the teacher is the key to what happens in social studies (and other) classrooms. Precisely how this key works and to what effect, however, has not been clarified. The NSF studies demonstrate that textbooks are also an important key to what happens in social studies classrooms.

We know some important things about those who teach social studies. The overwhelming majority of elementary teachers are female, while the vast majority of secondary teachers are male. Social studies teachers at all levels are quite experienced. Elementary teachers feel more qualified to teach reading and math than social studies and science. They also spend more time teaching those subjects. Junior and senior high social studies teachers feel qualified to teach their subjects and spend most of their time doing so. Only a few also teach other subjects. Social studies teachers are not very active in their professional associations, but they value other teachers as sources of information about new developments in their field. Teacher unions are not a significant factor in this respect, but they are a major influence on social studies and other teachers' professional lives, particularly in urban areas.

As parts of the social systems of their communities and schools, social studies teachers see socialization and preparation for the future as their primary aims. Moreover, their behavior in classrooms, related to the content of instruction and to classroom management, is consistent with this goal. Many teachers see and use subject matter as a vehicle for achieving these broader goals with students.

Major problems and needs for teachers of elementary social studies are related to materials and planning time. For secondary social studies teachers, lack of student interest and inadequate reading abilities are the prime concerns. Social studies teachers, especially at the secondary level, are less satisfied with their profession than are other teachers; and this is true at a time when teacher burnout and dissatisfaction appear to be widespread throughout the entire profession.

While these generalizations about social studies teachers can be made from the available research data, it is also true that there is considerable diversity among social studies teachers—even more so than among other teachers. They enjoy a high level of freedom, once the classroom door is closed, to teach social studies the way they want. Textbooks, training, and teachers' common views and attitudes work as centrifugal forces in shaping students' experiences in social studies. Freedom and diversity among teachers work as centripetal forces to create many variations and differences in those experiences. Sorting out the interplay between those two sets of forces and clarifying their impact on social studies classrooms and students will be an important research goal in the 1980s.

Chapter Six

Instructional Practices

Verna S. Fancett
Sharryl Davis Hawke

SOCIAL STUDIES CLASSES ARE NOT IDENTICAL across the nation, or even within a school. The diversity seems to spring not from what is taught, but rather from how it is taught. Case study observers saw evidence of this individuality in the social studies classes they observed. One wrote, "The approaches to the subject matter, the methods used, the content of the course, are blended together by the various teachers in many different ways ... [I]nstruction appears to cover the full gamut of approaches and methodologies" (Stake and Easley, 1978, p. 7:19).

Strategies range from "lecture and drill" to "free wheeling discussion and rap session," all depending on how the teacher judges a particular situation in a particular class at a particular time.

Teachers have great freedom to decide. In other matters they may have little choice, but decisions related to instructional techniques are almost entirely their individual and very personal domain.

What takes place in the classroom is the province of the individual teacher. The building administrators occasionally observe and evaluate, but teachers rarely intrude on one another. If a teacher chooses to lecture, run discussion groups, or confine himself to showing films, an unwritten rule seems to hold that others will say nothing about it (Stake and Easley, 1978).

Some teachers would like even more freedom; others see a need for more direction from the local or state level. Most are content with the way things are. As a result, they blend content and teaching styles in a variety of ways to teach the particular students they have in the best way they know how, based on individual preferences.

Student Grouping Practices

One characteristic of social studies instruction examined in the RTI survey was student grouping practices. From the survey data, a picture of the extent of large-group instruction, small-group work, individualized instruction, and ability grouping is fairly clear. Less clear are the reasons why these practices are employed.

Large-Group Instruction

At every grade level, social studies teachers spend at least half their instructional time working with the entire class as a group. This grouping practice is often found in grades 10–12, where it occurs more than two-thirds of the time (Weiss, 1978). But large-group instruction is not limited to the senior high level. Even in grades K–3, 59 percent of class time is spent in large-group instruction.

The incidence of large-group instruction takes on more importance when class size is also considered. Among science, math, and social studies classes, the largest are found in social studies at nearly every grade level. Average class size varied in the national survey from 24 students in grades K–3, to 28 in grades 4–6, to 30 in 7–9, and 27 in 10–12 (Weiss, 1978).

Small-Group Instruction

At no grade level do teachers use small-group instruction more than 15 percent of the time (Weiss, 1978). The amount of time spent in small groups is nearly the same across the grade levels, despite the common assumption that elementary teachers do more small-group work than secondary teachers. There is little in the data to explain the small percentage of time given to small-group instruction. One factor that is apparently *not* an explanation is "lack of assistance" (from a resource person or source). More than 60 percent of social studies teachers report that they "do *not* need assistance" (that is, inservice training or resource material) in small-group instruction (Weiss, 1978). Two factors that do seem restrictive are the lack of paraprofessional help in the classroom and the lack of adequate physical space in which to work with small groups (Weiss, 1978).

Small-group practices are thwarted not by the teacher's lack of knowledge but rather by the difficulty of managing a large group of students without help in confining spaces. To avoid the confusion, teachers opt for large-group, more easily controlled arrangements.

Individualized Instruction

In spite of the emphasis on large-group instruction and the almost casual use of small groups, social studies teachers do spend a considerable amount of time working individually with students. However, there is no evidence to conclude that this time meets the criteria of what is generally described as individualized instruction. Working one-to-one may or may not fit the pattern.

One impediment to individualized instruction is the belief of social studies teachers that materials to individualize are not available. Among 18 factors, "lack of materials for individualizing instruction" is considered the second most serious problem by social studies teachers. The problem is also considered serious by principals and state and district social studies supervisors (Weiss, 1978).

While teachers try to individualize, and seem to want to do even more, there is little in the current research base to guide them. Writing about this situation in a review of research, Martorella states:

There is evidence [from the field of cognitive style effects] that individuals vary in the ways in which they confront, process, and ultimately resolve thinking tasks. What specific implications this fact has for learning a variety of different social studies tasks across a variety of instructional designs remains, among other factors, to be established. From investigations into this area should come directions on how to begin matching students with appropriate instruction for given objectives (in Hunkins and others, 1977, p. 41).

Ability Grouping

Grouping according to ability exists in social studies instruction, though much less frequently than in mathematics and science (Weiss, 1978). In the elementary grades these groups are often based on reading ability and the difficulty of the material to be read. About 15 percent of elementary social studies classes are grouped according to some ability related to skills. Ability grouping is most common in the junior high, with almost a third of the classes grouped, and somewhat less common in the senior high, where about 24 percent of classes are grouped. Overall, about three-fourths of social studies teachers work with heterogeneous classes (Weiss, 1978).

When students are grouped, it appears that high- and low-ability classes are offered in about equal numbers. At the K–3 level, 7 percent of the classes surveyed by RTI were for high-ability students and 7 percent for low-ability. At the junior high level, the figures were 14 percent for high-ability students and 17 percent for low-ability. Figures were similar for grades 4–6 and 10–12 (Weiss, 1978).

Regardless of labels—tracks, levels, clusters, peer groups, pacings— grouping does exist, and it exists, teachers say, to help students. It may not always be done wisely or equitably, but it is done out of a conviction that for students to learn effectively and for teachers to teach effectively, students must be treated in different ways—sometimes even in unequal ways (Stake and Easley, 1978).

Teaching Arrangements

There is very little information in the survey and literature review concerning the use and effectiveness of various teaching arrangements in social studies instruction. This lack is curious considering the advocacy of team teaching and open space concepts in the 1970s. The most insightful data about the use of such arrangements comes from observations made by site observers in the case studies of school systems that employed such practices.

Single Teacher

From the case studies it is clear that social studies teachers, like other teachers, generally work alone. The classroom is a teacher's personal space, his or her territory, or turf. This attitude is common to most teachers and is often closely related to their sense of individuality. It is also tied to their feelings of responsibility toward their students, the need to control what happens so that students will learn. So strong is the feeling that the only "outsiders" most social studies students see in their classrooms are a very occasional guest speaker, a visiting dignitary in the district, or the principal or department chairperson who is required to file an observation report.

Cluster and Team Teaching

Cluster or team teaching and cross-discipline teaching occur in rare instances. Even when involved in a team situation, teachers still work alone, rotating responsibilities rather than sharing (Stake and Easley, 1978). It's a case of "you teach today and I'll teach tomorrow." The time made available in this every-other-day arrangement is used to do the housekeeping tasks, or to prepare for the next day's responsibilities. The use of team teaching for such purposes in part explains why teachers emphasize administrative and teacher benefits more than student benefits when discussing team teaching (Wiley, 1977).

Activity Centers/Open Space

The term "activity center" embraces a variety of instruction and uses. In one school it may be a completely free and open area where students chose optional activities during a scheduled or unscheduled period. In the elementary school, this type of activity center may be a converted classroom filled with "goodies" and supervised by a teacher. In other schools, the activity room may take the form of a social studies lab where students work on special projects, from map-making to the construction of a castle or the painting of a mural. Such centers are probably not common to most schools.

Also included in this category is the center constructed purposely to implement the "open space" concept. Here, both formal teaching and special activities can be accommodated. The instructional techniques of the social studies teacher in such an arrangement are often dictated by such things as noise level, movement of students from area to area, and perhaps most important, the ability of the teacher to cope with the lack of walls and structure.

Reactions to open space, where it existed in the case study schools, were mixed. An observer in one school summarized his observations:

Open space is a tolerated rather than an enjoyed feature of social studies instruction. The prevailing view is that the district administration decided on the open-space architecture and they had to plan within that concept. But two young teachers said that open space means no discussion in class. When class discussion is tried, the arm-waving, laughter, and oral disagreement have the potential to distract over 200 other students not involved. The good news about open space is that the students can see that all the other teachers cover the same content that theirs does. "It shows them we are not being unfair" (Stake and Easley, 1978, p. 1:52).

Given their choice of walls or no walls, social studies teachers probably opt for walls—the self-contained classroom. Where open space exists, it seems to be tolerated, at best. The favored arena for the social studies teacher is the classroom, certainly at the high school level, and most probably elsewhere.

Time Allotments

Administrivia

If we can assume that most beginning social studies teachers chose their profession out of a desire to teach, it is no surprise that they are often shocked and disillusioned by the amount of time they must spend on clerical tasks, what the bitter ones label "administrivia." And they are not alone. The so-called "veteran teachers" continue to rate this part of their jobs as most annoying and frustrating. As one said, "I always thought that the main goal of education was teaching kids; now I find out that the main goal is management" (Stake and Easley, 1978, p. 16:55). He was referring to the records he had to keep in order to support an individualized program. In his mind, this sort of bookkeeping might well be done by a clerk. His job was to teach.

The amount of time taken from teaching for clerical duties depends in part on the secretarial staff a district is able to support, the number of aides available, and the number of reports required by someone from above—the principal, the state, the federal government. Report requirements have mushroomed over the past few years, requiring more and more precise data on more and more subjects. How much actual time during a day, or more likely after school, is spent on this type of activity is difficult to estimate, even by teachers themselves, because it is sporadic in nature. There are peaks and troughs, depending on the time of the year when reports are due.

While a substantial portion of "administrivia" is necessitated by the bureaucratic requirements of the institution, the Goodlad study strongly suggests that not all "wasted time" is imposed by external forces. Much wasted time involves activities over which teachers do have control, "recesses that run too long, leisurely lunch period, and classes that wind up early" (*Denver Post*, October 11, 1981, p. 20a). The result, according to Goodlad, is that some elementary schools spend as little as 18 and a half hours a week on instruction, while others spend as much as 27 and a half hours. He also reported that some schools fritter away the final ten days of the school year, throwing away two of their 36 weeks.

Schools that devote more time to instruction use the day more efficiently, but they do not have longer hours, reported Goodlad. "They get down to business. A 15-minute recess lasts 15 minutes, not 30 minutes, and lunch is 30 minutes, not an hour. They don't spend the last half-hour of the day cleaning up, because they've found that it can be done in five or six minutes" (*Denver Post,* October 11, 1981, p. 20a).

Discipline

Discipline is a word known to all teachers. Most agree that discipline is necessary to learning, but their definitions of "discipline" vary considerably. Discipline may be used in a narrow sense to describe a teacher's behavior with a student who breaks a stated rule or requirement. It may also be used in a much broader sense to describe the whole process of "socialization," or preparing students to function effectively in the "school world," on the assumption that effective functioning there will lead to effective adult participation in other social institutions.

Putting it in a nutshell, most teachers seemed to treat subject matter knowledge as evidence of, and subject materials as a means to, the *socialization* of the individual in school. Socialized discipline was the *lingua franca* or "medium of exchange," within a school, transcending subject matter barriers (Stake and Easley, 1978, p. 16:24).

No data were found on the amount of time teachers devote to discipline—either in its narrow or in its broad sense. However, the national survey does provide some indication of how great a problem teachers perceive discipline to be. Interestingly, when compared with 17 other factors, maintaining discipline was considered by fewer than 8 percent of social studies teachers as a "serious" problem. Less than a third considered it "somewhat a problem."

The relatively minor importance of discipline seems to conflict with the increasing amount of attention given to violence in the schools in the past ten years. A possible explanation offered by the survey authors is that the question to which teachers responded in the survey related only to instruction in a specific subject area, not to school discipline in general.

Preparation Time

Lack of preparation time is seen as a serious problem in the elementary schools. In the secondary schools, about a third of the teachers expressed a great need for more time built into their work day to plan instruction. It is pertinent to note that there were significant differences in the number of subjects those teachers teach (Weiss, 1978).

For some, the five-class load consists entirely of one subject, say American history. For others, it may be three classes of American history, one of economics, and one of anthropology. The amount of preparation time required by a social studies teacher varies with those differences in responsibilities, but those in the latter category are not given extra preparation time.

Teaching

With the amount of time given to preparation, discipline, and administrivia, how much time do teachers have left for actual teaching? According to the teachers who responded in the RTI survey, social studies teachers in K–3 spend an average of 21 minutes per day on social studies. In grades 4–6, they spend 34 minutes (Weiss, 1978). Because these are averages, the figures include those teachers who "do" social studies in whatever time is left over after reading, math, and other things. It also includes those who have a special interest in social studies and give it a high priority. The averages show time spent on social studies to be substantially less than time spent on math but more than on science.

No figures are provided in the survey data on the average number of minutes spent at secondary levels in social studies classes, but class periods seem to range from 45 minutes to 55 minutes. The standard teaching load for junior and senior high social studies teachers is five classes in an eight-period day.

Another set of data collected by the national survey concerns the minimum number of mintues per day that districts specify should be spent on particular subjects at the elementary grades. The social studies percentages are about the same as for science, but somewhat less than for math. The average number of mintues specified ranged from 15 minutes for kindergarten to 39 minutes for grade six. The number of minutes for social studies is comparable to science but five to ten minutes less than for math (Weiss, 1978).

Use of Instructional Technology, Strategies, and Practices

Technology

If there is one common denominator of social studies classrooms throughout the nation, it is the centrality of curriculum materials in instruction. The Educational Products Information Exchange Institute (EPIE) reports that about 90 percent of classroom time, in both elementary and secondary schools, involves the use of curriculum materials. Most of this time is spent on commercially printed materials, mainly textbooks (EPIE, 1977). Less time is spent with teacher-prepared materials. In the initial EPIE survey, teachers reported that 30 percent of all the materials they used were locally produced. But a further breakdown showed that of this 30 percent, 52 percent were worksheets or exercises and another 27 percent were tests or progress evaluations (EPIE, 1977). It is in the production and use of these teacher-made materials that much of the use of educational machinery (ditto machines and overhead projectors, in particular) occurs.

Printed Material. Nearly all social studies teachers use at least one textbook. Even in grades K–3, where they are found least often, two-thirds of the teachers use them. The predominence of the textbook increases from grade four to grade 12, where only one teacher in ten uses no textbook at all. About half of all K–12 social studies teachers use a single published textbook or program; about a third use multiple texts (Weiss, 1978). Although size, region, wealth, and type of community seem to have little effect on the age of textbooks used, there is some indication that students in small schools are more likely than others to study from "old" texts (Weiss, 1978). Overall, about half the classes in the study were using books five years or older (Weiss, 1978).

Teachers are heavily involved in the selection of the textbooks they use, either individually or through committees of their peers. Only 3 percent of the schools responding reported no individual teacher involvement (Weiss, 1978). And most are satisfied with the text they are using.

While teachers like and use textbooks, their use of commercial printed supplementary materials is considerably less. EPIE's nationwide study reported that the largest number of respondents said they "neither have used, nor plan to use," any supplementary materials (EPIE, 1977). In summarizing various research studies, Wiley (1977) suggests that only about a quarter of social studies teachers use a variety of materials to supplement the text. Patrick and Hawke (1978, p. 9) conclude that "in general, most teachers make slight use of various published supplementary materials."

Machinery/Equipment/Instructional Aids. Although teachers rely heavily on printed materials to plan and implement their instruction, machines influence what is done and how. In the social studies classroom "the ditto machine" has made the chalkboard almost obsolete.

The most reliable means of instruction was dependence on the spoken word of a teacher equipped with a ditto machine. Even a shortage of textbooks could be better controlled if one had a ditto machine, ditto fluid, and access to a thermofax machine (Stake and Easley, 1978, p. 9:23).

Students in the Goodlad study also give evidence of the heavy use of worksheets. From upper elementary through high schools more than three-fourths of students reported using worksheets (Wright, 1980).

When asked in the national survey what needed improvement in the way of supplies, a third of the social studies teachers asked for a better supply of duplicating masters (Weiss, 1978). There are few data on the content of the worksheets, but an EPIE survey indicated that most worksheets are review exercises or tests (EPIE, 1977).

Two other machines tend to permeate social studies instruction, the film projector and its relative, the filmstrip projector. Both are considered indispensable and are used frequently by some teachers, although the film projector may be "a frustration, more bother than it's worth, in need of repair, or constantly breaking down in the middle of the film just when the real point is about to be made." The call for help to the AV room is a frustrating but accepted part of the instruction process. A study by the Agency for Instructional Television found that 60 percent of secondary social studies teachers use film at least once every two weeks (Fontana, 1980).

After the film projector and the filmstrip machine, the most commonly used instructional aide, according to the RTI data, is the overhead projector, which is used by almost half of the teachers at least once a month (Weiss, 1978).

Ditto machines, projectors, and overheads have been available in schools for quite some time. They are staples, and they are used. But teachers do not make use of more sophisticated and new machines. They seldom use records or tape recorders, and one out of two sees no need for the film loop, television set, or videotape recorder/player. The 1978 Weiss report showed almost no use of computers (Weiss, 1978).

Similarly, the computer is not a technological innovation toward which social studies teachers are gravitating, although there may have been important changes in the last several years, since the studies reported here were made. In the RTI study, more than three-quarters of K–12 social studies teachers said computers were "not needed" for their instruction (Weiss, 1978). A National Council for the Social Studies report on computers in social studies classrooms stated that while 74 percent of 974 districts surveyed reported using computers for instructional purposes, social studies courses used them far less than did mathematics, natural sciences, business, and language arts courses (Diem, 1981). The author suggests one explanation is social studies teachers' lack of training in the use of computers.

Commonly Used Instructional Practices

Knowing with *what* teachers teach, we move now to examine *how* they teach. Both the RTI survey and Goodlad's research explored this question. From these resources data emerge to show the predominance of three instructional strategies and a smattering of several other practices. We will deal first with the most commonly used practices.

Lecture. In the RTI survey, teachers were asked to describe the frequency with which they used various instructional activities. "Lecture" headed the list. Although not defined in the survey, it is unlikely that teachers interpreted the word lecture in the collegiate sense, that is, teacher exposition with little or no opportunity for student questions or challenges. Instead, it is likely that the word was interpreted as teacher "talk and demonstration," the terminology used in the Goodlad research.

Teachers reported using "lecture" frequently from the earliest grades through senior high, its frequency rising sharply from kindergarten to grade 12. Even in grades K–3, almost half of the teachers lecture "daily" to "at least once a week," and one out of five lectures daily. Only 27 percent of K–3 teachers never lecture (Weiss, 1978).

Dependence on lecturing increases steadily through the upper grades. Over a third of 4–6 teachers lecture at least once a week; a quarter lecture daily. In the junior high over half lecture at least once a week, a fifth daily. At the high school level the daily use rises to a third of the teachers. About two-thirds of social studies students listen to a lecture at least once a week; a quarter of them daily (Weiss, 1978). In the Goodlad study, students were asked to report on the instructional strategies they experienced. Ninety-three percent of upper elementary students reported use of lecture in their classes; the figure rose to 94 percent among secondary students (Wright, 1980).

According to the Goodlad study, the majority of students like the use of lecture or "teacher talk" (Wright, 1980).

Discussion/Recitation. Rivaling lecture as the most frequently used instructional practice is discussion. Again, it is impossible from the data to know exactly what discussion means to teachers who report using it frequently in their classes. Does the term indicate a true exchange of ideas or simply recitation with the teacher asking the questions and the students giving the answers?

Whatever its meaning, discussion is a popular strategy. Over half the K–3 teachers in the RTI survey and two-thirds of 4–12 teachers reported holding discussions on a daily basis (Weiss, 1978). In the Goodlad study of upper elementary and secondary students, about 80 percent reported that they experienced the practice in their social studies classes (Wright, 1980).

How do students feel about class discussion? In the Goodlad research, about 60 percent of upper elementary students said they like the practice. At the high school level, 85 percent of students said they like discussion "very much" or "somewhat." Only 4 percent said they disliked it "very much."

Individual Assignments. Students spend a great deal of time completing individual assignments—most often, writing answers to questions (Wright, 1980). Some of these assignments are completed in class, usually following a teacher lecture or class discussion. However, other assignments are the basis of homework. In part, individual assignments are used to enable students to learn new information. They also serve to reinforce previous learning or give additional practice in skill development. However, a third function is to help the teacher assess student learning.

Less Commonly Used Instructional Practices

Inquiry/Discovery Learning. In the 1960s, the "new social studies" movement, much touted by academics and heavily supported by federal funding, attempted to engage teachers in the use of inquiry or inductive teaching methods. From the RTI survey, the case studies, and the literature review, we have evidence of the extent to which this instructional practice is used some 15 years after the major push to establish it in classrooms across the nation.

Only 5 percent of junior high and 20 percent of senior high social studies teachers regularly try to teach the scientific analysis of social problems (Stake and Easley, 1978). Strategies and techniques used by social studies teachers at the secondary level are not commonly derived from the inquiry-oriented, scientific approaches used by social scientists. This finding supports earlier reports that the extent of teacher awareness about new social studies materials was fairly high, but the use of the materials was low (Wiley, 1977).

A major conclusion drawn by site researchers is that teachers do not tend to be natural inquirers themselves. They give small place in their teaching strategies to the development of systematic modes of reasoning. Where such practice is found, it may be more a part of the teacher's nature than the result of recent trends and curriculum development.

Values Education. Following on the heels of the "new social studies" movement was the emphasis in the late 1960s and early 70s on values in the social studies classroom. Although a rather amorphous idea taking different instructional forms, the intent of most values education was to help students clarify their own and others' value positions. From the case study research emerges the most insight into the use of values education in social studies classes.

It appears that the most pervasive reason for not using some form of values education is the fear of negative reaction from the community. Teachers and administrators worry that the encouragement of questioning can stimulate controversies, which may not be wise. It is safer, most believe, to stick with the facts and leave values clarification to those who wish to take the gamble.

As a result, where values teaching does exist, it is more apt to be inculcation than clarification. Even this is not common; teachers simply stay away from the issue (Stake and Easley, 1978). Therefore, the handling of controversial issues, including values, is apparently not a major problem in the social studies. However, some evidence suggests that social studies teachers actually have more freedom in dealing with controversial issues than they realize and use.

Community/Experience-Based Instruction. At no grade level is there frequent use of field trips as an instructional practice. Eighteen percent of K–3 teachers take a field trip at least once a month; 53 percent take some trips; and 19 percent never go on field trips. After the third grade, the use of field trips drops continuously through the twelfth grade (Weiss, 1978).

The infrequent use of field trips may be the result of increasing pressure to spend more time on what some teachers call the 3 C's—course, content, and coverage; the problems of supervising large groups of students; disapproval of teachers in other disciplines who resent their students "missing class"; and lack of funds. Although the NSF site researchers did find examples of concerted, well-planned experience-based instruction, it was rare; where it did exist, it lacked the support of most teachers.

The work of Newmann (1975) and others indicates the many possibilities offered by experienced-based instruction. For example, internships in a multitude of government and civic agencies, performed by serious students who want to combine the knowledge of the past with the urgency to live the present in a productive way, have become common in many schools and many social studies programs. These internships enable social studies students throughout the country to combine service with learning in the most practical and powerful way—on the job. In some cases they earn social studies credits toward graduation; in others, they simply become involved in applying what they have already learned in order to learn more.

Unit or Course Projects. Social studies students are apt to be involved in a project or the preparation of a report at least once a month, except in grades K–3, where projects and reports are used about half as often; and 25 percent of the teachers there never use them (Weiss, 1978).

Simulations. Simulations, including role-play, debates, and panels are used by most teachers less than once a month, with one in five teachers indicating that they are never used (Weiss, 1978).

Modules, LAP, and Programmed Instruction. Less than three out of ten social studies teachers ever use programmed instruction, and most of those use it once a month or less (Weiss, 1978). Where "packages" are found, they are usually part of the schoolwide effort to implement an objective-based curriculum. While some teachers find packages to be a boon for students who lack self-direction, others find them uncreative, restricting ability to switch approaches as the need arises, or to take advantage of each "teachable moment." Some complain that such instruction is antisocial, placing students in isolation, away from the social interaction that should be a major characteristic of social studies teaching and learning. Proponents of these techniques criticize the way teachers use packages, not the packages themselves.

Contract Learning. The use of contracts is not common in social studies at any grade level. When asked to rank 16 instructional techniques according to their frequency of use, teachers placed contracts next to the bottom, just slightly ahead of computers (Weiss, 1978).

Evaluation Practices

Whatever instructional techniques teachers use to convey new information and build understandings among students, most teachers regard some sort of evaluation of student progress as essential. Evaluation helps the teacher to assess student progress and students to evaluate themselves. The RTI survey and Goodlad's research give us some indications of how prevalent evaluation is and what techniques of evaluation are most commonly practiced.

Teacher-Made Tests. According to RTI data, students frequently take tests or teacher-made quizzes. Forty-four percent of teachers give a test at least once a week (Weiss, 1978). Forty percent of K–3 teachers never use tests, but that figure drops drastically in grades 4–6 where only 4 percent never use them. More than half of secondary teachers test in some form at least once a week (Weiss, 1978).

Most of the tests used in the classroom—as opposed to workbooks and exercise sheets—were developed by the teacher, often using questions from another test or from the textbook or teacher guide that accompanied the textbook. These *teacher-made tests* were much more closely attuned to what actually occurred in class and as part of the laboratory work or homework than districts' objectives-based tests, the publishers' tests, the criterion-referenced tests or standardized tests—and to be sure, there were very few of these more formal instruments to be seen in any of the schools (Stake and Easley, 1978, p. 15:15).

Frequent testing is seen as an important way of teaching and making certain that students have learned. It is also viewed as a good way to accomplish one of the major goals of teaching—the socialization of students. Of testing and socialization, Stake and Easley write:

Although formal testing did not seem to satisfy much of the teacher's need for knowing what the student knew, testing did seem to assist in socializing students and maintaining control over them. . . . Testing was relied on to motivate the students. The information provided by tests seemed mainly used in the justification of past decisions and the allocation of further opportunity (Stake and Easley, 1978, p. 15:23).

Studies indicate that teachers have very limited expertise in the field of evaluation. Their techniques tend to be confined to objective and essay tests, class discussions, and student papers, all based on content objectives (Wiley, 1977).

Recitation, Homework, and Exercise Sheets. Although teacher-made tests represent the most common "formal" means of student testing, student evaluation is common during recitation periods. Stake and Easley write in their summary of findings from the case studies, "the dominant form of testing over the last fifty years [has been] recitation, an informal kind of testing rather than examination, a more formal kind" (1978, p. 15:14).

Assigning Grades. The frequency with which tests are administered increased rapidly after sixth grade, as we have noted. This is compatible with the increasing use of competition as one moves from kindergarten to grade 12. Students may be graded on a number of things—knowledge, attitudes, performance—all of which may or may not be a result of social studies teaching. With the recent emphasis on "basics" and "competency," social promotion, if not disappearing, is at least coming under scrutiny. "You get what you earn" is becoming more and more the bottom line in grading. This is particularly important in light of parents' concern about grades.

[S]ome parents were suspicious of teachers' grading practices. Visits to schools and calls to teachers were made by some parents to obtain reassurance of the teacher's sensibility and impartiality. The teacher usually would turn to tests, exercises, and work samples to explain the grade, but the exact rationale of the teacher's interpretation remained unclear (Stake and Easley, 1978, p. 15:20).

Contrary to what students throughout the ages may have thought, grading is probably not a task that social studies teachers relish. Many regard it as "the" most unpleasant and disturbing part of their job. It is common to hear teachers say, "I love to teach, but I hate to give grades!" This reflects their dedication to their students, their desire to do the "right" thing for each of their charges, and their fear of doing damage with a stroke of the pen.

Standardized Tests. Standardized tests are used more frequently in grades K–6 than in grades 7–12. In the RTI survey, half of the school districts used them in K–6 classes and only a third of the districts in 7–12 classes (Weiss, 1978).

More than half of the elementary schools reported using standardized test results in social studies to report to teachers and parents, place students in remedial classes, and revise curriculum. Almost as many use the results to place students in classes for the gifted or to diagnose and prescribe for individual students. In secondary schools the results for social studies are used by more than half of the schools to report to teachers. Almost half report to parents. Other uses are infrequent (Weiss, 1978).

Factors Influencing Teachers' Choices of Instructional Practices

There has been little change in instructional practices over the years. Teachers of social studies continue to teach as they have always taught, probably as they themselves were taught. They are receptive of change, but guarded, skeptical, and cautious.

In the eyes of social studies teachers, innovations come and go with regularity; technology rears its ugly head with more and more machines to master and tame; ideas flow like fountains from educators isolated from the day-to-day reality of the classroom; directives come from someone in an office somewhere—all suggesting what should be done in the classroom. But teachers, throughout it all, sense that they will continue to be the ones who decide to accept or reject, to encourage or block, or simply to tolerate.

Personal Competence and Beliefs

Personal Beliefs. Probably the most powerful of all influences is the one that is self-imposed by the nature of the teacher as an individual. Teachers draw and depend on their personal strengths, selecting those activities with which they feel most comfortable and effective. Decisions that social studies teachers make about how to teach are based on what they feel is best for their students and on how those students learn most effectively.

Preservice Education. Preservice education is a likely source of teachers' personal beliefs about instructional effectiveness. Apparently it has some influence. About a third of teachers at grade levels 4–12 and a somewhat higher proportion at grades K–3 consider their college courses to have been "very useful" sources of information. About half of teachers at all grade levels consider the courses to have been at least "somewhat useful" (Weiss, 1978).

Conclusions drawn by Shaver and others (1979a) about the generally discordant relationship between classroom teachers and university subject matter specialists suggest that the usefulness teachers ascribe to preservice education must come from subject matter, not instructional learning. Comments from teachers often suggest that their preservice courses emphasized the "theoretical" while the classroom demands the "practical."

Administrative Influences

Because teachers are employees of a school district, it is reasonable that at least some of their choice of instructional methods would depend on the wishes of the school board and administration. Stake and Easley site observers suggest that classroom teachers and administrators are isolated from each other; as a consequence, teachers do not see superintendents and district personnel as "informed" or sufficiently "concerned about conditions in the classroom" (Stake and Easley, 1978). Nevertheless, certain expectations are set by these "inadequately informed" administrators. "Most teachers . . . felt powerless to take action that would challenge the boundaries" (Stake and Easley, 1978, p. 19:17).

The other side of the coin is that administrative boundaries do not impinge much on teachers in their own classrooms. "At most sites the teacher had a great deal of leeway as to what would be covered in the course of study and as to how time would be spent in class . . ." (Stake and Easley, 1978, p. 19:17). Thus, administrative restraints and expectations are set, but for the most part the sanctity of the classroom is protected and teachers do not feel greatly constrained.

School Climate

Whatever a teacher's preservice education, previous inservice experiences, or district policies, he or she works in an individual school with an ambience of its own. In the words of one site observer,

The schools have lives of their own, existing as organisms exist, to "be on with it," perpetuating themselves and protecting against assault from without. . . . The philosophy and style of the principal and the traditions and social structure within a single school probably have most to do with the educational program there (Stake and Easley, 1978, pp. 2:23, 2:20).

What happens to the teacher in these autonomous organisms? According to Stake and Easley, they become institutionalized or at least socialized into the school's climate.

Although difficult to define and quantify, it appears that the prevailing school climate, as exemplified by administrators, students, teachers, and the physical plant, is a powerful influence on teachers' choices of instructional practices. Any movement to "reform" or change teachers' instructional practices must take into account the factor of school climate and recognize its restraining and supportive potential.

Community Influence

Because schools are locally supported institutions, community expectations and wishes have always weighed prominently in educational decision making. The influence of community expectations on teachers' choices of instructional practices takes place early on—in the hiring of teachers. From all the case study observations, Stake and Easley concluded that:

Teachers had been carefully selected to fit the community and that teachers were anxious not to put children or parents in anguish—so some occasionally went as "far out" as the community, the parents and the youngsters would let them, but seldom further (Stake and Easley, 1978, p. 16:25).

This is not to say that all teachers were alike. What seemed to emerge in each community was a comfortable mix of "relatively stern socializers and relatively liberal socializers" (Stake and Easley, 1978, p. 16:25).

Within the seldom-defined but generally understood expectations of the community, teachers choose their instructional methods. Most parents seem to agree with the heavy dependence on the textbook, lecture, and recitation. They learned with such methods when they went to school. They did not use simulations, role play, and open-ended discussion; therefore parents are likely to regard such innovations as "fun and games." Teachers can avoid questions about their teaching practices by simply avoiding the nontraditional practices.

The back-to-basics movement has helped demonstrate how closely teachers and lay persons tend to think alike in matters of instruction. While some teachers have protested back-to-basics as a restraint on their choice of instructional practices, most have no complaint and indeed support the movement. Stake and Easley found that in discussing back-to-basics, a "large number of teachers said something like the sixth-grade teacher in River Acres who answered, 'Back? We never left!' " (Stake and Easley, 1978, p. 13:35).

Research Findings

Theoretically, one influence on teachers' choices of instructional materials would be findings from research on cognition and teaching methodology. Nowhere in the sources reviewed was there direct information on how much teachers use such information to make decisions. In the national survey, 40 to 45 percent of social studies teachers considered professional journals a "very useful" source of information, but it is unclear how much, if any, of the perceived usefulness is related to research findings.

One limitation on a teacher's use of research findings in making instructional decisions is the nature of such findings. For the most part, research related to instructional effectiveness has netted few concrete answers—answers that are definitive and that suggest immediate applicability by teachers. In summarizing the research reviewed for a 20-year period, Wiley writes:

A large proportion of the effectiveness research conducted in the social studies falls under the heading of research on instructional methods and much of this focuses on various methods labeled "critical thinking," "inquiry," and the like. Most of this research shows no significant differences between critical thinking methods and so-called traditional methods . . . (Wiley, 1977, p. 9).

Martorella, in another summary of research on cognition, reaches the same conclusion but also addresses the question, "Does research tell us anything about the effects of instruction on cognitive variables?"

Research can always tell us something. The issue is how useful the answer is. And much of the potential usefulness of the answer depends upon how you perceive it (Hunkins and others, 1977, p. 45).

Martorella goes on to say that there are some clear-cut findings concerning instructional variables. "Much is already known about sequencing and organizing instruction to facilitate a narrow range of cognitive outcomes. There are a number of specific models and guidelines suggested by research for teaching facts and concepts" (Hunkins and others, 1977, p. 46).

In summary, of the factors that influence teachers' choices of instructional practices, the most powerful are the climate of the school in which the teacher works and the expectations of the community in which the school is located. The influence of these sources in large measure shapes the thinking of teachers and ultimately forms their personal beliefs about which practices are most effective and practical. Pre- and inservice training, behavioral objectives, and research may play a role in shaping choices, but the messages from these sources are filtered through community expectations and school climate. Those practices that prove compatible with climate and community are the ones most likely to enjoy long-term use.

Conclusion

We know much about how social studies is being taught in the U.S. today. We know, for example, that most social studies instruction, regardless of grade level, is conducted in large-group arrangements, led by a single teacher rather than by teams or in clusters. Aside from instruction, much of teachers' time is occupied by administrivia, discipline, and preparation.

The most common tools of the teacher's trade are textbooks, dittoed worksheets, and films, which are used in lecturing, leading recitation, and making assignments. Teachers do not make much use of "innovative" practices. They evaluate through teacher-made tests, recitation, and homework assignments.

In making instructional decisions, teachers rely most heavily on the expectations of their school and community. Because of this, the public and the school administration support the traditional methods the majority of teachers use most of the time.

Part Three

The Future of Social Studies

Chapter Seven

Six Problems for Social Studies in the 1980s

SPAN Consultants and Staff

MUCH OF A POSITIVE NATURE CAN BE SAID about the schooling of Americans. We have a high level of literacy, a high and increasing average number of years of schooling, students who show a zest for growth in certain aspects of their lives, many fine educational materials, a broad base of public support for education, and many creative and dedicated educational personnel at all levels of education.

Nevertheless, there is widespread criticism of the state of education in the United States—on the part of the public and many educators, as well as SPAN consultants and staff. The focus of SPAN, as of many other recent studies of American education, has been on the shortcomings and on the potential for improvement of education. While the heralding of positive accomplishments might be good for our collective ego, and perhaps has been neglected in recent years, only an analysis of short-comings and a vision of potential are likely to bring about improvements.

In its broad review of the state of social studies, Project SPAN has identified six major problems, which serve to focus its formulation of desired states and recommendations for social studies.

Problem 1: Student Learning

Many students leave school without the knowledge, skills, and attitudes that are important and desirable outcomes of social studies programs. In addition, many students do not like or value social studies as much as other subjects.

It appears that the knowledge, skills, and values of social studies students are inadequate, and that there has been little or no improvement in recent years. With few exceptions, a comparison of NAEP scores from 1969 to 1976 and 1972 to 1976 and MAT (Metropolitan Achievement Test) scores from 1970 to 1978 reveal the following results for social studies knowledge, skills, and attitudes: little or no improvement for elementary students, no improvement and slight declines for junior high students, significant declines for high school students (NAEP,

1978a; NAEP, 1978b; Copperman, 1979). Reference to a different data base—review of research—leads to similarly discouraging news related to attitudes and values. Programs designed to improve students' political attitudes, values clarification abilities, and levels of moral reasoning have not demonstrated substantial success (Ehman, 1977, 1979; Leming, 1979; Lockwood, 1978).

Finally, students do not like social studies very much and do not believe the subject is very important to their lives after school. While there are exceptions, most of the research evidence from questionnaires and observations points to widespread lack of student interest and motivation (Wiley, 1977; Stake and Easley, 1978; Weiss, 1978; Wright, 1979). Student lack of interest, indifference, and boredom seem to be prevalent in social studies classes, especially at the secondary level (Stake and Easley, 1978; Shaver and others, 1979a).

Clearly, lack of student interest and learning in social studies is a major problem to be addressed in the 1980s. Why does this problem exist? Explanations may lie in descriptions of the five other problems facing social studies education.

Problem 2: The Culture of the School

The culture and organization of schools, especially at the secondary level, focus much of the energy of teachers and administrators on matters of management and control rather than on the teaching and learning of social studies—particularly the teaching and learning of higher-level thinking skills, participation skills, and democratic values.

This problem is not unique to social studies. The power, stability, and complexity of the school and classroom culture were largely underestimated or ignored by curriculum reformers in the 1960s and 70s. This reality, however, pervades, influences, and often hinders academic pursuits—particularly efforts to bring about change—in the elementary, junior, and senior high schools. This important conclusion from the classic studies of the last decade (Sarason, 1971; Jackson, 1968; Cusick, 1973; Lortie, 1965; Goodlad and Klein, 1970) has been confirmed by recent studies (Stake and Easley, 1978; Serow and Stike, 1978) and analyses (Holman, 1980; Grannis, 1980; Anderson, 1982).

Schools, especially at the secondary level, are characterized by a high degree of specialization, hierarchy, transient relationships, work based on coercion or extrinsic rewards, and major emphasis on institutional maintenance, which often conflict with high quality service for "clients." The central force underlying the school culture is its commitment to socialization—preparing young people to be good students (to earn good grades) and good citizens in adult society, with emphasis on existing norms and practices (Shaver and others, 1979a). Within the school, this means teaching students to respond promptly to bells, to respect school property, and to obey school rules. Within the classroom, this includes teaching students to pay attention to directions, to be quiet during class presentations, to get assignments in on time, to respect the rights of other students, and to obey the teacher's rules.

Consistent with these efforts at socialization, teachers and administrators devote considerable time and energy to maintaining order and discipline and managing groups of students. Often, the teaching of subject matter either is sacrificed—to take attendance, to issue late slips, or to stop a student from daydreaming—or it is used as a management device; for example, by using class time to have students write answers to the questions at the end of a chapter (Stake and Easley, 1978). In addition to such overt efforts at socialization, most aspects of the "hidden curriculum" convey similar messages—the physical setup of the classroom, the teacher's benevolent authoritarian posture, and the authority structure of the school. Teacher-to-student interaction is the dominant mode of communication rather than a combination that includes, for example, student-to-student or student-to-teacher interaction (Marker, 1980; Fielding, 1981).

Many other aspects of the school culture that affect students do not necessarily enhance academic learning. These include the sheer size of many schools, fragmented time schedules, and the nature of tests and grading systems. While teachers, administrators, and community members may share a commitment to the effective socialization of students (Stake and Easley, 1978) and the maintenance of a benevolent authoritarian structure, their diverse positions in the system sometimes result in conflicts in immediate goals. These conflicts surface clearly in the planning of field trips, for example. A teacher would like to have students engage in a community-based activity, but the principal is worried about transportation and lawsuits, the assistant principal about accurate attendance records, and the counselor or other teachers about students missing other classes.

In addition to the problems related to the organization of the school, many elements of the student subculture turn attention away from organized learning efforts—including friendships, sex, sports, and other extracurricular activities ("Sex Rated Below Friends," 1979). The fragmentation of effort may be intensified in a large school where it is impossible to relate to and know everyone personally (Panel on Youth, 1974). Development of a humane climate and sense of community in large schools may also be more difficult, thereby hindering identification with the school, turning attention away from the central goal of schooling, and possibly encouraging vandalism and violence.

While all curricular areas feel the restrictions and demands of the culture of the school, social studies is unique in the degree to which it finds its learning objectives in conflict with the culture. Although social studies is charged with teaching the fundamentals of democracy, schools are authoritarian systems. The highest-level skill and value objectives in social studies call for students to become active, participating decision makers—yet there is little opportunity within the school setting for these skills to be practiced and evaluated. Consequently, while teachers of other subject areas may find their teaching objectives limited by the school culture, social studies teachers must confront with their students the ever-present discrepancy between what they preach (democratic principles) and what they are required to practice.

Problem 3: Teaching Practices

Instruction in social studies is generally characterized by lack of variety in teaching methods and evaluation practices, by limited kinds of learning experiences, and by inattention to the implications of educational research.

The dominant methods of instruction in social studies are lecture and discussion/recitation based on textbooks (Weiss, 1978; Stake and Easley, 1978; Shaver, Davis and Helburn, 1979b, p. 151; Patrick with Hawke, 1982; Fancett, 1982). In a typical social studies lesson, the teacher assigns students a section of the text to read, follows with a recitation based on the reading, informally lectures on the topic, engages students in a discussion that involves students' answering questions, or has students complete written worksheets in class or as homework. While some of these materials include decision-making and valuing questions, little social studies instruction engages students in using a variety of materials or participating in active experiences such as role plays, action projects, or inquiry activities, either in or out of the classroom. Most instruction in social studies occurs in large-group settings with little use of small-group or individual approaches (Weiss, 1978).

The evaluation practices most commonly used in social studies classrooms tend to reinforce the dominant instructional practices. The predominant evaluation procedures are objective and essay tests, assessment of participation in class discussion, and grading of student papers (Wiley, 1977). An examination of the kinds of tests, homework assignments, and class discussion tasks commonly used indicates that teachers evaluate students on only a very narrow range of variables, primarily low-level cognitive operations such as recall of information and application of concepts (Rappaport, 1978). Generally avoided in evaluation are synthesis and evaluation, reasoning skills, and critical and creative thinking. Although paper-and-pencil tests *can* measure higher-level thinking operations, most teacher-made tests in fact do not (Stake and Easley, 1978).

In recent years, there has been considerable research on learning and student development, but few social studies teachers are aware of or influenced by the results of such research (Wiley, 1977). While Shaver (1979) and others have compellingly pointed out the dangers in trying to apply the results of educational research to classroom practice, some recent research syntheses suggest useful principles for instructional improvement. One such example is an article by Peter Mortorella (1979) that offers several research implications for instruction; for example, "The use of questions organized in some logical sequence in teaching has a significantly positive effect on learning compared to alternative approaches. . . . In addition, increasing the amount of time given for students to respond to questions tends to improve the quality of response" (pp. 599–602; see also Rowe, 1978).

Responsibility for the failure to make use of such research lies in part with researchers who do not effectively communicate the results and implications of their work to teachers, in part with teachers who are unreceptive to the work of "those people in ivory towers," and in part with the lack of opportunities for researchers and teachers to interact with each other. Whatever the reasons, most instruction in social studies (and other areas) is not based on or responsive to students' cognitive and social developmental needs and abilities, as these are revealed by research.

There are many reasons for teachers' heavy reliance on textbooks, for the lack of variety in their instructional practices, and for their inattention to new research. Although some teachers complain about the reading levels of texts, most teachers generally like to use textbooks (EPIE, 1976; Klein and others, 1979). Textbooks help teachers organize the various bodies of knowledge they teach, particularly if they must teach disciplines other than those in which they have formal training. In an era of concern about "back-to-basics" and proficiency testing, the text is an acceptable, concrete resource for student learning. While many materials incorporating varied learning activities have been developed, few preservice or inservice training programs have emphasized practical ways to use these techniques. Teachers told case-study investigators that their resource people "largely did not know the realities of their classroom situations" (Shaver and others, 1979a, p. 16).

Teachers who know about and are predisposed to use a variety of instructional practices may find it difficult to do so. Seldom do teachers have role models to emulate, having studied under college professors who primarily lecture. New teachers' models are generally restricted to other teachers on their school faculty, most of whom have a very small repertoire of strategies. Difficulties are also posed because many of the instructional practices that involve students in active learning require a substantial amount of preparation time (Wiley, 1977). Teachers also express concerns about the frustrations of students who cannot deal with the tasks involved in active learning (Stake and Easley, 1978).

Perhaps the most important reason for teachers' use of a limited range of activities is fear that inquiry and action-oriented practices will make the management and control of students too difficult. Teachers' primary concerns "center on classroom management and socialization—

the matters that must be handled to survive each day and [to] gain and maintain respect in a social system made up of other teachers, administrators, parents, and students" (Shaver and others, 1979b, p. 152). In general, the strategies teachers use are "those that are considered to be safe in the classroom, the school, and the community. The more innovative teachers seem to sense how far out they can go and do not cross that line" (Fancett and Hawke, 1982).

Problem 4: The Curriculum

The social studies curriculum—courses, materials, and content—is focused primarily on specific facts and broad conclusions from history and other social science disciplines rather than on critical-thinking skills, social science concepts, values and attitudes, and social participation. The curriculum, moreover, is not based on student developmental needs and does not emphasize important societal issues and effective participation in the social world.

The social studies curriculum today is based on a pattern of topics and subjects that was established more than 50 years ago (Lengel and Superka, 1982; Hertzberg, 1981). The content and organization of these courses are not likely to encompass ideas and skills focused on the current and future needs of students and society (Wiley, 1977; Shaver and others, 1979b). Instead, they focus on topics, facts, places, time periods, and broad conclusions of history, giving little emphasis to science concepts, critical-thinking skills, and social participation. Perpetuating these curriculum characteristics are commercially published curriculum materials that present information to fit traditional expectations (Patrick and Hawke, 1982).

The traditional curriculum gives little recognition to the developmental characteristics and needs of students. Subject matter is placed at various grade levels with little regard to what is known of children's cognitive and social development. Courses in world history or world geography, for example, are taught to seventh-graders, who are engaged in an intense period of *self*-discovery.

Over the years, particularly the past 15 years, the curriculum has been challenged by many attempts to bring social science, current issues, and social concerns into the curriculum. The Wiley literature review (1977) contains nine single-spaced pages of topics and subjects that have been adopted by one or more schools, including legal education, multicultural education, career education, and consumer education. These topics have been thought by many to be worthy, legitimate additions to social studies, and considerable attention has been given to infusing their messages into existing courses. However, with some exceptions—attention to ethnic diversity in particular—schools have made only temporary commitments to such topics, replacing them after a trial period with traditional courses or gradually reducing the time devoted to them. The curriculum has not facilitated the inclusion of these courses.

From a practical standpoint, there are few incentives to change the curriculum pattern and many forces weighing against change. Laws in 41 states require that American and/or state history be taught at elementary or secondary levels, or both. Civics or government is required in 31 states at one or both levels (Henning and others, 1979). Perhaps the strongest force supporting the status quo is tradition. With a 60-year history behind it, the present curriculum pattern is comforting to social studies teachers, administrators, and parents, most of whom experienced the pattern themselves as students (Lengel and Superka, 1982).

Aware of existing laws, examinations, and traditions, publishers produce commercial materials that support the status quo. Paul Goldstein, who made a critical study of textbook development, writes, "The surest, least costly way to succeed with new materials is to follow the patterns successfully established by materials already in use" (quoted in Patrick with Hawke, 1982). The result is limited alternatives for teachers; if they wish to break the curricular pattern, they must write their own materials. Few choose to do so (EPIE, 1976).

What we have, then, is not a nationally imposed curriculum, but "a locally accepted nationwide curriculum" (Shaver and others, 1979a, p. 24). Despite numerous calls to reorganize the social studies curriculum, few comprehensive K-12 curriculum organizational schemes have been advanced, and none has been adopted widely (Schneider, 1980).

Problem 5: The Profession

Parts of the social studies profession, in varying degrees, are characterized by considerable disagreement on the most important goals and objectives of social studies and by a decided lack of direction, satisfaction, opportunities for professional growth, and constructive interaction among the various participants.

Precollege teaching is an isolating activity. Teachers generally work alone with their students; only rarely do they work together in team-teaching arrangements or on cooperative, education-related tasks. Although about half of the social studies teachers in the RTI study felt that lack of articulation between teachers of different grade levels was a problem (Weiss, 1978), few attempts to achieve coordination were reported in the case studies (Lengel and Superka, 1982).

At teaching levels other than elementary and secondary there is also little interaction. The relationship between teacher educators and other college professors is characterized by limited communication, some distrust, and lack of mutual credibility; a similar relationship exists between college professors and precollege teachers. Although publishers of social studies materials communicate with some teachers, most teachers never have an opportunity to work with curriculum developers. Nor do they come into contact with educational researchers, except possibly as subjects in studies; seldom are they asked to consult on decisions about what questions to research—consultation that might improve research and make it more relevant to teachers' interests and needs and to school realities (Shaver, 1979).

A major factor contributing to the lack of constructive communication is the existence of isolated subcultures within the profession— groups of elementary teachers, secondary history teachers, teacher educators, and curriculum developers, to name a few. Interaction among the various subcultures is inhibited by differences in needs, values, and reference groups, as well as by the well-established pecking order among different levels of education, which places graduate teaching at the top and elementary teaching at the bottom. Members of the various subcultures are most often brought together in settings that reinforce the "pecking order"; for example, precollege teachers take college classes to learn from college professors, while college professors seldom participate in classroom teachers' sessions at professional meetings. The differences in interest and values among members of the various subcultures and the pecking order phenomenon clearly overshadow the common concern for effective social studies education, dividing the profession into special-interest cliques.

For teachers, lack of opportunity for constructive interaction is aggravated by limited opportunities for personal growth, advancement, and renewal. The proliferation of articles in both professional and popular magazines concerning teacher frustration and "teacher burnout" points up the acuteness of this problem for all teachers. Another reason for burnout that emerged from the NSF case studies is the myriad demands placed on teachers to meet diverse student needs and burgeoning requirements to keep records and write reports.

At all levels of the profession there continues to be confusion about the basic purpose of social studies, which is reflected in the continuing debate about what social studies is, or should be. At the same time, pressures from the back-to-basics movement and directives for accountability are forcing local educators to define their goals and objectives for social studies. Meanwhile, new topic areas continue to bombard the field, leading to situations such as the one described in an NSF case study:

Unfortunately, social science is too often seen as a synonym for a collection of courses—often lacking a sequential development—a course here and a course there (Stake and Easley, 1978, p. 10:8).

We are left with the impression of a profession diffused in its goals and directions, lacking constructive channels of communication, and possessing little sense of "profession" among its various subcultures.

Problem 6: Public Support

There is insufficient public support for and understanding of social studies programs that are balanced, judicious in responding to special interests, supportive of democratic values, scientifically and educationally sound, and relevant to the present and future lives of students.

Social studies suffers from a variety of conflicting attitudes and responses on the part of the public. On the one hand, there is strong public support for the teaching of certain social science and history subjects. On the other hand, there is evidence that social studies is not seen as very useful—for example, as being less useful for later life than English, mathematics, commercial courses, shop, and extracurricular activities (Gallup, 1978).

Still another aspect of the public's low esteem for social studies is the decline in attention and support given to social studies in the elementary grades. Much of this neglect is attributable to public concern for reading and computation skills. Substantially less time is devoted to social studies than to reading or math in the elementary grades, particularly in grades K-3 (Weiss, 1978; Lengel and Superka, 1981). Informal reports indicate that in some districts elementary social studies programs are fighting for their very existence.

Like today's students, adults do not recall that social studies was useful to their lives after school. While people may lend verbal support to citizenship goals, the overwhelming majority of the public spends little time in citizenship pursuits (Marker, 1980).

When strong public interest in social studies is shown, it is often manifested by a small group focused on a particular topic or subject. Special-interest groups have made intensive efforts to secure more space in the curriculum for certain topics or subjects and to inject certain views—often without consideration for how those topics and views fit into the total social studies curriculum. Some special-interest pressures on the curriculum are directed toward censorship. While sex education and evolution controversies have sometimes been directed toward social studies instruction, censorship battles in social studies have been staged more commonly over values education, patriotism, and teaching about religion.

Thus, the social studies profession has failed to communicate effectively the characteristics of a broad and balanced social studies program and why it is of crucial importance at all levels of education. This failure has resulted in the narrow view of social studies held by many people. Social studies professionals have seldom made clear to the public the importance of social studies in helping students examine political and social issues; understand the influence of such problems as classism, racism, and sexism on their lives; value diversity in an interdependent world; resolve personal problems; and make rational decisions about their private and public lives. Thus, social studies retains public support for only a small portion of the kind of program most educators agree is desirable.

Potential For Future Progress in Social Studies Education

SPAN consultants and staff, like many other observers of the educational landscape, believe there is great potential for the improvement of education in general and of social studies in particular.

Despite the shortcomings of many schools and programs, many others are demonstrably better. Throughout the nation are compelling examples of outstanding teachers teaching in creative and effective ways. Some model curriculum programs have been designed to keep social studies vital and effective. These programs have been implemented in ways that please teachers, students, and parents. Scattered across the country are schools that have found practical ways to decrease management and control functions so that students can experience more flexible class and out-of-class learning. If some teachers and schools are accomplishing these goals, we have good reason to believe other schools can make comparable improvements.

In addition, a significant number of students today are excelling beyond the achievements of their predecessors, although student achievement in social studies is not uniformly as great as we would like. Similarly, even though student valuation of and interest in social studies fall short of the ideal, some students do like social studies and find it worthwhile. Students also show great zest for learning and participating in other aspects of their lives—sports, music, friends. Thus, we are not struggling with a "defective" input—we simply need to use students' natural enthusiasms in their social studies learning.

We also take hope from the fact that public education still retains considerable public support. Since 1950, per-pupil expenditure, *in real terms* (adjusted for inflation), has *tripled* (Historical Statistics, 1975; Statistical Abstract, 1980). Admittedly the public, particularly officials, are more carefully scrutinizing public expenditures for education, and schools are being held increasingly accountable. But public support is still there and will probably continue for the foreseeable future.

Finally, despite what initially appears to be great resistance to change, education as an institution is capable of change. Whereas 100 years ago less than 5 percent of the high school age population attended school (with all the rest already out of the system and at work), now nearly all—90 percent—stay in school long enough to earn a high school diploma (Coleman and others, 1974). This has required many accommodations in the operation of public schools. Students with academic or behavioral problems, who formerly would have dropped out, now stay in school. For the most part, schools have been successful (though not always eager) in finding effective programs to deal with such students. More recently and more swiftly, with the passage of HB 94-142, millions of handicapped students who once would have been placed in special schools or allowed to stay out of school are now being provided educational opportunities in regular classrooms. The fact that education has been able to move from an institution for the elite to an institution for the masses helps allay fears that no change is possible.

Progress in education seems not to come in the rapid, dramatic manner that we see in science and technology. Yet the potential is as real. By learning from the experiences of past reform efforts and squarely facing our current problems, we can utilize the unrealized potential of students, teachers, schools, and the institution of education itself to bring about not just change, but indeed progress.

Chapter Eight

Desired States for Social Studies

SPAN Consultants and Staff

IN UNDERTAKING TO SPECIFY "DESIRED STATES" for social studies, Project SPAN does not intend to picture a state of affairs that, once achieved, will remain forever perfect—and static. Paradoxically, desired states should be viewed as achievable goals and, at the same time, directions for moving toward goals that are forever changing and receding. Human thought and imagination can never perceive the ultimate ends of human endeavor.

The desired states are described in the present tense, as though they might exist in the near future—when the fragile wisdom of the present has already interacted with the uncertainties and realities of the future to create conditions that reflect progress while pointing to still better states to be accomplished.

The picture presented here is based on certain assumptions that could turn out to be erroneous. For instance, we assume that, for some time in the future, there will continue to be in the United States a typical setting in which most students advance from kindergarten through the twelfth grade; that the configuration of elementary, middle, junior high, and senior high schools will be similar to that of the past few decades; that most education will take place in public school classrooms in which student-teacher ratios vary between 20:1 and 30:1; and that school curricula will continue to offer reading, writing, mathematics, natural science, social studies/social science, and other familiar subjects. Any or all of these assumptions might be overturned in the next 10 or 20 years, by electronic technology or other technical or social metamorphoses. The desiderata described here assume no such radical changes; within the existing framework, they are radical enough.

Desired State: Student Learning

Students in elementary and secondary schools throughout the country are actively, enthusiastically, and successfully engaged in learning social studies. Appropriate to their respective grade levels and developmental abilities, the vast majority of students are learning the central concepts and relationships in social studies and the factual knowledge needed to develop those concepts

91

and relationships. They are applying this knowledge as they examine social issues and develop the critical thinking, valuing, and social participation skills needed to be effective participants in society.

Students in elementary and secondary schools are learning fundamental knowledge in social studies. This knowledge includes major facts, concepts, generalizations, and theories from history, political science, geography, economics, sociology, psychology, and anthropology, in addition to well-selected and closely-related knowledge from humanities and philosophy. Students also display a keen and deep awareness of cross-cultural and global perspectives as they learn about many social issues. In addition, students display ability to reflect historical perspectives, understand current issues, and consider future orientations. Their levels of understanding depend on and relate to their particular levels of cognitive development; their learning of social studies, in turn, facilitates their cognitive development from concrete to more abstract forms of thinking.

Students are able to examine historical and current social issues critically, displaying such thinking skills as critical questioning, locating and analyzing information, making comparisons, and interpreting and evaluating data. Students can deal with written, oral, visual, and graphic data. As they progress through their social studies classes from kindergarten through grade 12, they learn more complex applications of these skills. They are also learning decision-making skills, such as defining a problem or dilemma, considering alternatives, and choosing and justifying decisions; and interpersonal and valuing skills, such as identifying the values of others, becoming aware of their own values, seeing things from other people's points of view, and working effectively with others.

Social studies programs are enhancing students' understanding of and commitment to the basic democratic values of our society, such as justice, freedom, equal rights, diversity, and responsibility. Students use the critical thinking and valuing skills learned in social studies to translate these values into specific definitions and policies and to resolve value conflicts in their personal and public lives. Students actively participate in the community and society and show the desire and the abilities needed to continue that participation after leaving school. In the development of democratic values, social studies shares responsibilities with other subject areas, the school administration, the media, the family, and other agencies of society. Paralleling these shared responsibilities, social studies educators take initiative in communicating with other agencies about these goals and the methods of achieving them.

As a result of the appealing and clearly stated goals of social studies and the varied and effective means of accomplishing the goals, students consider their social studies classes to be interesting, important, and useful both in their lives as students and in their future lives and careers. Elementary students and teachers consider social studies enjoyable and

important parts of their school life. At the secondary level, the popularity of social studies is evident; students enjoy their social studies courses
and believe they are relevant.

Desired State: The Culture Of The School

The culture and organization of elementary and secondary schools reinforce
and enhance the goals of quality social studies programs. The rules, decision-
making processes, interpersonal relationships, management procedures, and
physical settings of the schools reflect a positive, humane climate; but less
positive realities of the political, economic, and social world are also
examined, thereby providing students with a context and experiences that
help them develop into effective and responsible participants in society.

Social studies is taught in schools that are large enough to afford
good services and facilities, yet small enough to foster a sense of
community. Elementary schools have up to 300 students, secondary
schools from 600 to 1,200 students. These schools have a good deal of
staff and parent consensus about the major goals of schooling, so that
students receive consistent messages about their obligations and rights.
Rules are consistently enforced, and high expectations are held for the
performance of all students.

Positive relationships between staff and students are developed as
teachers of different subjects work in teams with responsibility for a
given group of students; as teachers spend time with students in
activities in addition to instruction—in sports, music, counseling, trips,
and dining together—and as teachers and students cooperate in maintaining the school and improving its facilities.

Communication and cooperation among students are ensured
through emphasis on cooperative learning activities (for example, teamwork in academic learning and group research projects), service to
others (peer tutoring, peer counseling, service to community agencies),
and group-based service to the school itself (teams of students responsible for care of the school's equipment, for hosting visitors, for production of assemblies, and for maintaining bulletin boards and displays of
art in common areas). Flexible scheduling and grouping patterns enable
students to spend long periods of time working on projects such as
renovation of a home, oral history of the local community, production of
video tapes, research, service, and advocacy outside of school. Teams of
teachers working with separate student groups each have enough
autonomy to pursue their studies, without frequent interruptions due to
administrative concerns.

Students at the secondary level participate in the governance of the
school through a variety of activities designed to elicit serious student
input: class study and discussion of issues facing the staff and administration, assemblies highlighting issues of school policy, surveys of
student opinion, and spontaneous discussions with staff regarding

school policies. These activities supplement and give substance to formal mechanisms such as student councils.

Teachers are accountable for enhancing student learning. They are also expected to participate in the communal aspects of school, such as assemblies, clean-up, extra-curricular programs, and student counseling. Teachers are aware of how the school's organizational features and "hidden" curriculum can be modified to improve school climate.

There are frequent opportunities to publicly confirm a sense of community within the school: for example, in regular assemblies, display of class pictures, school songs, public recognition of outstanding achievements of students and staff members, attempts to help school members facing difficult personal issues, and celebration of events of special significance to ethnic groups in the school.

The school's sense of community, unity, and caring among students and staff does not suggest that standards of excellence in learning occupy a low priority. On the contrary, standards of excellence for everyone doing one's best are a fundamental unifying factor, pursued within a supportive and cooperative climate, in which teachers and students learn to deal with the tension they may perceive between attempts to build cohesion and attempts to achieve individual competence. Similarly, the ethic of cooperation and unity is not allowed to stifle critical inquiry and criticism of the school itself, an area in which social studies classes have a special responsibility.

Desired State: Teaching Practices

Social studies teachers use a variety of instructional practices and instructional materials to achieve the various objectives of their social studies programs. Enlightened by up-to-date findings of educational research and learning theory, they strive to make instructional practices and materials compatible with the needs and capacities of individual students and with the particular learning tasks at hand. While not all teachers are equally skilled in using a wide variety of instructional practices, very few rely primarily on lectures, recitations, and a single textbook. Social studies teachers use a variety of evaluation methods, designed to assess the progress of students, to diagnose the learning problems of individuals, and to assess and improve the social studies program.

Social studies teachers use the most appropriate strategies and practices to develop important concepts, critical thinking skills, valuing skills, and social participation. To the extent possible, teachers also select and use the practices and strategies most appropriate to the learning styles and development levels of the students and to their own teaching styles. With young students, for example, social studies teachers make extensive use of pictures and hands-on materials because of students' need to learn from concrete experiences. Many social studies teachers incorporate peer learning activities into their instructional practices, thereby giving students opportunities to learn from one another. These practices are consistent with research findings on cognitive learning and student development.

Teachers commonly use a variety of didactic strategies to help students retain cognitive content. Advanced organizers are frequently used to help students structure their knowledge. Deductive and inductive strategies are used to teach concepts and generalizations. Opportunities for practice and experimentation with concepts are provided to help students internalize these concepts. Periodic practice and reinforcement activities are used in both concept and skill development. Information from a variety of media are used in all these activities, including written narratives, graphs and tables, photographs, films, filmstrips, TV, and tapes. Textbooks are still commonly used as an important source of organized information and knowledge, but are rarely treated as the ultimate and sole source of truth. Primary-source and case-study materials are used extensively to teach critical-thinking and value-analysis skills. Roleplays and small-group discussions are frequently used in teaching value issues. To develop participation skills, teachers have students work individually and in groups in the classroom, school, and community on various projects. These activities include conducting surveys, conducting interviews, observing everyday experiences, working in businesses, and engaging in civic activities. While many teachers incorporate these out-of-school experiences into their regular classes, some schools have special courses in which students' primary experiences are in the community.

Teachers use a variety of evaluation practices to determine student progress and achievement of the major objectives of social studies programs. With the help and support of administrators and supervisors, needs assessments, diagnoses, ongoing formative evaluations, and periodic summative evaluations are conducted as an integral part of instruction in social studies. Valid and reliable tests—short answer and essay types—are used widely but not exclusively. Analysis of student work and systematic observation are also used to pinpoint strengths and weaknesses in student knowledge and skills. Interviews and attitude surveys are among the methods used to assess program strengths and weaknesses and to determine areas in need of improvement. While there is a considerable amount of evaluation activity, none is done without careful and prior thought as to how the results will contribute to student learning and to improvement of the social studies program.

Desired State: The Curriculum

The social studies curriculum in elementary and secondary schools enables students to understand and function in the real social world. Although specific programs and organizational patterns vary throughout the nation, each school's curriculum is based on a substantial amount of attention to each of the generally agreed-upon major goals of social studies: knowledge from history and the social science disciplines, critical thinking and interpersonal skills, values and valuing skills, and social participation. Moreover, the social studies curriculum attends to each of these dimensions: the needs and abilities of students, the concerns of society, and the nature of the disciplines (subject matter); past, present, and future perspectives; and individual, societal, and global aspects. Each curriculum rests on a clearly defined rationale, with explicit objectives, a nonrepetitive pattern of topics and courses, and appropriate materials and activities. Local needs and resources are considered as individual curricula are developed, revised, and implemented on a K–12 basis, and there is congruence between a school's stated social studies curriculum and its actual practice.

The social studies curriculum throughout the nation reflects a healthy balance of unity of purpose and diversity of approaches. The ultimate purpose of social studies is to help students understand and function in the real social world—to be effective as individuals in society and to be thoughtful, responsible, and active participants in our democratic society. The major goals of social studies flow directly from that purpose and include an integration of the key elements of good social studies curricula. Detailed goal statements direct substantial attention to the major goals of knowledge, skills, values, and participation. Social studies progams throughout the country reflect a synthesis of the best elements of the long-standing traditions of citizenship transmission, social science, and inquiry into social issues. A balance and integration of goals and approaches is not necessarily reflected in each unit, textbook, or even course, but it is achieved on a K–12 basis in different ways by different districts.

At the heart of each school's social studies curriculum is an operative statement of the program's goals and objectives. Written in a manner and level of specificity appropriate for that school's needs, this statement of program goals and instructional objectives is directly related to the major goals of social studies which guide the profession and provide a framework for program courses, materials, and activities within the district. Preceding the development of the goals and objectives statement, or derived from it later, is a statement of social studies rationale which provides the philosophical underpinning for the goals and objectives and relates directly to the ultimate purpose of social studies—to help students understand and function in the real social world. These rationale statements contain positions about the nature of the individual, the nature of society, the nature of values, the nature of knowledge, and the nature of learning.

Based on statements of rationale, goals, and objectives, the curriculum provides balanced attention to the areas of knowledge, skills, affective development, and social participation. Knowledge is drawn from the major facts, concepts, generalizations, and theories of all the social sciences and history, and is presented to students through topics that interest students and allow them to sense the complexities of the social world. Continuing attention is given to analyzing current social issues and trends that reflect the realities of social injustice as well as justice, conflict as well as harmony, diversity as well as unity. Skills, particularly those leading to higher-level critical thinking, are specified and stated in terms of outcomes which are measurable by a variety of techniques. From kindergarten through the twelfth grade, attention is placed on the development of attitudes of students which will help them become more effective social participants. Included in the curriculum are opportunities for students to actually participate in their social world as well as to study about it.

The pattern of topics and courses that the social studies curriculum follows is based on the logic of the social science disciplines from which content is drawn, the developmental needs and abilities of students, the central concerns of society, and the resources available to the local school. The places, events, periods, and situations that students study are chosen and placed in the curriculum according to their contribution to the teaching of essential skills and concepts of social studies as well as to their broad understanding of the history of humankind. Students' study is apportioned among global, national, state, local, and self-related topics at all levels of schooling. There is a mix of topics and issues drawn from the past and present, with projections into the future.

Significantly influencing the selection of topics and courses in the social studies curriculum are the interests of students as well as their cognitive and social development abilities and needs. Although the research on student development does not provide definitive answers to questions of curriculum organization, attention is paid to findings on how students learn. This leads to placement of certain kinds of topics at certain grades. For example, topics that lend themselves to study via concrete objects and experiences are placed at the elementary level; topics dealing with the self are studied during early adolescence; topics providing a wider look at institutional systems are studied in later high school years. At all levels, topics are included that allow students to put their skills to use in practical situations and to receive feedback from the social environment.

Each school includes a study of major social issues and concerns in the social studies program. The particular issues and ways in which they are incorporated into the curriculum vary. Some schools have several separate courses focusing on current problems or social issues. Others deal with these issues within history or social-science-based courses. In any case, students are given opportunities to examine, research, and discuss key societal concerns from local to global settings.

The social studies curriculum also reflects the reality of the local school's resources. As much as possible, curricular topics and courses are chosen to utilize teachers' strengths and interests. Included as a part of social studies' curriculum resources is the world outside the classroom.

Teachers regularly use community resources such as museums and government offices in social studies instruction, calling upon private and volunteer support to supplement school funding. While continuing efforts are made to provide appropriate and up-to-date materials, the social studies program works within budget realities by long-term planning and careful use of expenditures for materials.

Recognizing the importance of curriculum materials in instruction, the social studies staff places high value on the search for and selection of appropriate and effective social studies materials. Materials represent a variety of instructional modes. In both textbooks and other kinds of supplementary materials, a mix of learning styles and teaching methods is available. At each grade level, students are exposed to instruction not only from the printed word, but also from photographs, paintings, music, speeches, realia, maps, globes, and charts. No single method or style of presentation dominates the use of materials. Their content similarly reflects the goals and objectives of the social studies program, with emphasis on stimulating student thinking rather than memorization.

While the development of curriculum is a multi-layered process that includes participants both within and outside the school, it is the teacher who brings life to the curriculum and makes it an effective vehicle in the preparation of students for participation in the social world of their present and future. It is the teacher who decides how the topics and skills are taught to students in the class, who selects and implements material, and who moves social studies instruction beyond the classroom walls.

Desired State: The Social Studies Profession

All members of the social studies profession—teachers, supervisors, teacher educators, history and social science professors, curriculum developers, publishers, and others—have a common commitment to social studies education and work cooperatively toward its improvement. They also share a unity of purpose and belief in major goals for social studies. Although members of the profession are united in their efforts to achieve these goals, to strengthen social studies' role in school curriculum, and to improve students' learning experiences, diverse views on how to accomplish these goals are welcomed and given fair hearing and are reflected in practices throughout the profession. Working together, members of the social studies profession help to maintain high standards of performance, press for continued professional growth for all members, and provide constructive opportunities for members to interact among themselves, with professionals in other areas of education, and with noneducators.

Among the members of the social studies profession, there is a strong sense of shared purpose and commitment to the major goals of social studies and to continual improvement in social studies education. There is a healthy diversity of approaches to achieve those goals.

Advocates of these approaches have carefully articulated their approach by developing a rationale statement, learning objectives, scope and sequence, examples of curriculum materials, and classroom activities. This development has been encouraged by the intellectual climate within the profession, which fosters the creation of new ideas and provides forums for their review. When new ideas are put forth, they are carefully examined for intellectual soundness, practicality, and potential for enriching social studies instruction.

A positive rapport has developed among social studies educators through frequent and sustained working experiences. All recognize their shared assumptions and interests while also recognizing the ways in which their roles are naturally divergent. There is respect for each educator's role in social studies education, and the expertise of various segments of the profession is sought when solutions to new problems are needed.

Ways in which members of the profession work together are numerous. For example, classroom teachers assist teacher educators in structuring and conducting methods courses. Teacher educators work with teachers in "action research" efforts aimed at identifying specific ways to modify classroom practices to facilitate learning. Supervisors function as consultant-coordinators in bringing together and articulating the concerns of teachers. Supervisors communicate these concerns to administrators and state department personnel and help to formulate and interpret responses to teacher concerns. Supervisors and campus-based teacher educators work together to use the resources of learning psychologists, social scientists and historians, curriculum developers, and lay persons to improve social studies instruction. The local, state, regional, and national organizations of social studies educators support and enhance the relationships of all segments of the profession. Their conferences and publications are seen as support services to local efforts and individual teachers.

In view of the importance of curriculum materials in social studies education, the relationship among curriculum developers and publishers and teachers, supervisors, teacher educators, and disciplinarians has been strengthened. Curriculum materials development, whether by special projects, commercial publishers, or local district personnel, is conducted by individuals who are well informed about and attuned to the alternative social studies approaches. Appreciating the value of diverse approaches to achieving the major goals of social studies, developers and publishers provide the alternative materials which are needed to implement the various approaches. Others in the profession work with commercial and special-project developers to ensure that information about products reaches teachers who are seeking particular kinds of materials. Where local needs dictate unique approaches, special development efforts are supported by private and public funding efforts.

In the selection or development of curriculum materials, as in all other phases of their profession, social studies educators are acutely aware of the importance of keeping in mind the overall purpose, the general rationale, and major goals of social studies. At the heart of all professional activities there is awareness and periodic review of the goals and objectives of social studies programs and of the rationales that support and direct those activities. Constantly considered are questions such as: What are the needs of individuals and of society that social studies can help to meet, and what do we know about the nature of individuals, society, knowledge, values, and learning that will both limit and facilitate our efforts to meet those needs?

Professional growth of social studies educators, another important dimension in social studies education, is fostered through both group and individual opportunities and activities. Growth opportunities for staffs or groups of educators are provided by districts, states, and national agencies. In these endeavors, usually taking the form of inservice sessions and workshops, attention is on the current and future needs of staff. Needs are determined by teachers and supervisors who work together to design and sometimes conduct the sessions. An important function of these inservice experiences is to help career teachers keep current on new findings in student development, on new knowledge generated in the disciplines, and on new ideas for curriculum and instructional practices.

Not all professional growth is generated through group experiences. Recognizing that adults, like students, have different needs, the profession has focused attention on the importance of providing each teacher an opportunity to grow in a way that is personally meaningful. For teachers and other educators, renewal opportunities include role exchanges, travel, personal research, creative materials development, conference attendance, professional writing, and structured reading time. Administrators are well aware that such individualized renewal opportunities are critical in preventing burnout and dropout among career educators and give appropriate administrative and financial support for these efforts. However, individuals assume responsibility for their own growth experiences and work with appropriate administrators and available resources to carry out their plans.

Having joined its members in a commitment to building and maintaining a strong position for social studies in the school curriculum and to continually improve students' learning experiences, the social studies profession has also taken the initiative in engendering public support for social studies instruction. Individuals and groups of social studies educators have opened and sustained various channels of communication with a variety of individuals and groups. From informal discussions with parents to carefully arranged presentations to community organizations and national audiences, public support has been sought and gained. Through open and positive communication, social studies educators have not only helped the public understand and support social studies' purposes, they have also gained valuable insight and knowledge from persons outside education about ways in which to improve social studies instruction.

Underlying the commitment and activities in the profession is a recognition that social studies education is not static. The profession embraces the dynamic nature of social studies and responds by constantly reviewing while analyzing and growing. Unity of purpose is sought while diversity of approach is welcomed. Communication is open. New ideas are viewed as challenges. This orientation provides the common focus and energizing spirit that keep social studies in the forefront of elementary and secondary students' education.

Desired State: Public Support

School boards, parents, citizen groups, and the general public actively support social studies programs in the schools. They are aware of the nature and importance of social studies in the education of young people, and many are involved in helping to provide meaningful experiences in social studies in their local schools. Social studies teachers and supervisors are engaged in frequent and constructive efforts to inform and involve the public in social studies. Most members of the public realize that many aspects of social studies lead to controversies that can contribute to the growth of good minds. They are supportive of efforts to present all sides of controversial issues both in the schools and in public forums.

Under the leadership of the National Council for the Social Studies, the local and state councils and district social studies supervisors have regular mechanisms for communicating with the community about the aims and practices of their social studies programs. The nature and significance of social studies is often explained and demonstrated to parents, school boards, and other members of the lay public. In addition, members of the local community are actively involved in social studies programs as guest speakers, resource people, advisory group members, and facilitators of student experiences in the community. Indeed, the public shares with teachers and other educators a sense of responsibility for helping students learn social studies. While various special interest groups still work at the local, state, and national levels to achieve their special goals, they are restrained by teachers, administrators, and the pubic to recognize that special viewpoints have limited roles in the successful implementation of a broad, comprehensive social studies program.

Chapter Nine

Recommendations for Social Studies in the 1980s

SPAN Consultants and Staff

HAVING DESCRIBED THE CURRENT STATE OF SOCIAL STUDIES and suggested desired states to which social studies educators might aspire, Project SPAN faced the most difficult task of all—formulating recommendations for moving toward those desired states. One suggested approach resulted in a very short set of recommendations:

1. Study the description, analyses, and diagnoses contained in the reports on the current state (or states) of social studies. Decide on the extent to which you agree with those reports and decide for yourself how they can help you understand and improve the state of social studies from your own perspective and position.

2. Study the desired states as proposed by Project SPAN. Decide the extent to which you agree and disagree with them·and how you would modify them to set an agenda for yourself to improve social studies.

3. Considering your own position, perspective, abilities, resources, and influence, decide how you can act to improve social studies in your state or district.

End of recommendations.

The SPAN personnel wanted to go further than this, but they were caught between the impossibility of specifying recommendations for particular individuals in particular positions and the high level of generality that must attend efforts to speak to educators in general. We decided to attempt the latter route, presenting general recommendations and speaking as much as possible to the particular roles of ASCD members. Thus we have omitted the (still general!) recommendations contained in the full SPAN report that are directed to authors, publishers, university professors, researchers, and persons in funding agencies, even though some of these persons are counted among ASCD members.

The recommendations are organized to parallel the six desired states. Thus, each set of recommendations is introduced by a brief summary of the desired state to which the following set of recommendations relates. The verb "can" rather than "should" is used in the recommendations, suggesting that these recommendations are possible while avoiding an overly-prescriptive tone.

For each desired state, two or more major recommendations are presented, which specify the broad tasks that need to be undertaken to move from our current state to a desired state. Following each major recommendation is a series of specific recommendations addressed to identified audiences, suggesting how various segments of the profession can contribute to implementing the recommendation. The order in which the audiences are listed generally reflects a judgment of which audience has the greatest responsibility or the greatest potential for implementing the recommendation.

We are not suggesting that the recommendations will be easily accomplished, nor that they can be accomplished in a short period of time. Rather, they are the beginning of incremental changes that will improve the state of health of social studies education. Members of the profession can assess the usefulness of the recommendations and begin to implement those that have the most potential for bringing about desired changes in their particular circumstances.

Student Learning

Desired State

Appropriate to their grade levels and abilities, students are enthusiastically engaged in learning the concepts and relationships of social studies and the factual knowledge needed to develop those concepts and relationships. They are developing critical thinking, valuing, and social participation skills.

Recommendations

Student learning comes as a result of achieving the other five desired states. Therefore, no specific recommendations are given beyond those that are related to those desired states. These recommendations follow.

The Culture of the School

Desired State

The culture and organization of elementary and secondary schools reinforce the goals of social studies programs. Rules, decision-making processes, interpersonal relationships, management procedures, and physical settings of schools all reflect a positive, humane climate that mirrors political, economic, and social realities.

Recommendations

A. Project SPAN recommends that social studies educators assume leadership in efforts to increase awareness and knowledge of the culture of the school and its impact on learning.

The first step toward minimizing the negative aspects and effects of school culture on student learning and moving toward the desired state of having the school culture enhance and reinforce that learning is to *study* school culture and its impact on teaching and learning. Awareness and understanding will not guarantee the constructive change, but they are prerequisites to such efforts. It is important for all persons involved in education—students, teachers, administrators, and others—to become more aware of the powerful influence of their particular school cultures on the education and lives of students. Examining and understanding social systems and cultures is a central aspect of social studies. It is, therefore, reasonable for social studies educators to lead these consciousness-raising efforts in the 1980s. Significant contributions to these efforts can be made by each of the following groups.

1. *Social studies teachers* can use the school and its culture as content for the social studies curriculum. Teachers in all grades can use examples and topics drawn from the culture, political system, and sociology of the school to illustrate social studies concepts such as authority, decision making, subcultural groups, rules and laws, rights and responsibilities, physical environment, and work roles.

2. *Social studies supervisors, chairpersons, and other school administrators* can lead efforts to identify the "hidden curricula" operating in their schools and determine the degree of congruence between explicit learning objectives and the implicit messages and values presented to students. Those aspects of the hidden curriculum that can be examined include strategies used by teachers to maintain order and control in the classroom, methods used in social studies instruction, relationships between teachers and administrators (especially in regard to making and enforcing school rules), the implicit messages conveyed by the organization of the social studies curriculum, and the physical structure of the school.

B. Project SPAN recommends that social studies educators initiate and support efforts to change aspects of their school cultures that inhibit and conflict with the realization of the goals of quality social studies programs, while striving to establish, maintain, and extend activities that reinforce those goals in students' school lives.

School cultures are not easily changed. Schools will probably never become models or laboratories of democracy in action. Some steps can, however, be taken toward making the cultures of schools more conducive to developing thoughtful, responsible participants in our democratic society. In most schools, for example, it should be possible to move toward more openness, better communication, and more extensive cooperation between and among students, teachers, and administrators, while fostering appropriate degrees of autonomy, decision making, and personal achievement. Because social studies is centrally concerned with human relationships, social institutions, citizenship, and cultural change, social studies educators can contribute much to these efforts. Specific changes in school culture can best be determined and approached on a school-by-school basis.

The following examples indicate some actions that educators in various roles can undertake that would represent important changes in the cultures of many schools.

1. *Social studies teachers* can initiate cooperative learning activities to foster goals not often reinforced by the dominant use of traditional, individual classroom activities. These cooperative activities can include team learning, group research projects, group service projects, peer tutoring, and peer learning and counseling. These activities may also include teamwork on specific projects, including interdisciplinary activities and programs in which students study topics from several subject areas. Many current societal issues provide opportunities for interdisciplinary approaches—for example, the social and scientific aspects of technology, energy, and the environment.

2. *Principals and other building administrators*, with encouragement and suggestions from social studies teachers, can organize and conduct a variety of schoolwide activities designed to build and enhance a sense of community and caring among the students and faculty. These activities can also emphasize social participation by students, the development of humane values, and critical thinking. Examples of such activities are assemblies, clean-up campaigns, fund-raising campaigns, and celebrations of special events, including those significant to different ethnic groups.

3. *Social studies supervisors* can work with building principals and other administrators to encourage and reward teachers for using interdisciplinary and cooperative learning activities in their programs. This can be done by providing inservice programs, modifying schedules, providing ample planning time, and giving recognition for these efforts.

4. *School boards and superintendents* can plan to keep school sizes small wherever possible. Social studies teachers can support these efforts by stressing the importance of small schools to the development of a sense of community and identity. At the elementary level, a reasonable limit is about 300 students. At the secondary level, between 600 and 1,200 students may be the optimal size.

Teaching Practices

Desired State

Social studies teachers use a variety of instructional practices and materials to achieve the objectives of their programs. With knowledge of educational research and learning theory, they strive to make practices and materials compatible with the needs and capacities of students and the learning tasks at hand. Very few teachers rely primarily on lectures, recitations, or a single textbook. They use a variety of evaluation methods to assess the progress of students, learning problems, and the social studies program.

Recommendations

A. Project SPAN recommends that social studies educators make systematic and continuous efforts to broaden their repertoire of instructional practices and materials, with a view to providing a variety of approaches suitable to particular learning tasks and to the needs and capabilities of particular students.

Considering the hours, weeks, months, and years that students and teachers spend in school, it can be argued that a variety of teaching practices and materials is valuable just to prevent monotony. But there are still stronger reasons for using various teaching practices and materials. First, there is the fact that different students respond to different types of stimuli, and that most students learn best by experiencing a variety of approaches. Second, there is the consideration that student learning depends considerably on matching learning experiences with stages of cognitive and affective development. Finally, in social studies there is a wide variety of objectives—knowledge, skills, values, and participation—that can best be learned through varying and tailoring teaching methods to learning tasks. The history of past reform efforts indicates that every social studies teacher will not suddenly use a wide range of teaching practices skillfully merely because there are good reasons for doing so. It is possible and important, however, for each teacher to make a determined effort to broaden and improve these practices, even if on a modest, incremental basis. Social studies teachers need to make the personal commitments to do this, and administrators, teacher educators, and others need to provide them with the help and support necessary to accomplish these efforts.

The following actions are examples of the contributions that various groups of educators can make toward widening the range of instructional practices teachers use in social studies.

1. *Social studies teachers* can assess their own instructional strengths and weaknesses and make personal commitments to learn or improve on at least one new instructional technique each year. Attention can be directed, for example, to new discussion strategies, role playing and simulations, community-based activities, use of media, concept-development strategies, surveys, and case studies.

Social studies teachers can provide their students with at least one special, long-term (several days or several weeks) learning experience each year that relates to important concepts, skills, valuing, or participation objectives and that is likely to be the kind of experience many students will remember and talk about years later. Depending, of course, on the teacher and student, many types of activities could comprise such experiences—Bloom calls them "peak learning experiences"—including social action projects, simulations and role-play activities, peer-learning and cross-age teaching programs, community-based learning activities, and individual or group research projects.

2. *Social studies supervisors* can plan and conduct inservice programs that focus on the use of different instructional strategies and practices. These programs can include materials and activities that teachers can readily use in their classrooms. Wherever appropriate, teachers who are particularly skillful in a specific practice should help conduct these programs.

Social studies supervisors can also take advantage of opportunities to engage their teachers in programs that by their nature invite the use of different instructional practices. These types of programs include law-related education, values education, local history, community studies, multicultural studies, and global studies.

B. Project SPAN recommends that social studies educators take advantage of the diversity that already exists among faculties in order to provide students with a variety of teaching models, styles, and practices in social studies.

While lecture and recitation based on a textbook clearly characterize the dominant teaching practice in social studies throughout the nation's schools, there is also considerable diversity among the teachers in individual styles of teaching, personalities, interests, values, and areas of expertise. Recently a fair amount of research in education has focused on identifying and matching teaching styles with students' learning styles. The ideal may be to provide a precise match of teacher and learner, but the practical implementation of that goal seems far away. A more attainable objective may be to realize, clarify, and extend the diversity that already exists within the social studies faculty in a school and to utilize that diversity to maximum advantage so that each student has opportunities to experience a variety of models and styles of teaching. The following are some specific actions educators can take to encourage that practice in social studies.

1. *Social studies teachers, principals, counselors, and others* responsible for helping students plan their schedules can encourage students to take social studies from different teachers so that they can benefit from various teaching models, styles, and instructional practices.

2. *Principals, supervisors, and others* responsible for hiring new social studies teachers can make pointed efforts to build and maintain social studies faculties comprised of teachers who represent a diverse range of models and instructional styles.

C. Project SPAN recommends that social studies educators develop and use a variety of evaluation techniques to assess student learning and their social studies programs.

One of the major barriers to using different teaching practices and working toward various instructional objectives is the dominant use of factual recall tests as the major method of student evaluation. Teachers have not been provided with a variety of useful and practical techniques for evaluating student progress in developing critical thinking skills, social participation, and values. Primary accountability for both students and teachers still rests with grades based largely on written tests that stress recall of facts and on the scores from standardized achievement tests. Less emphasis needs to be placed on gathering standardized test data in social studies, unless it is used directly to make program evaluations and decisions. More emphasis needs to be placed on other means of gathering evaluative data, including attitude surveys, content analysis, observation, student self-evaluation, and oral examinations. Moreover, evaluation needs to be focused more on diagnosis of student needs and evaluation of programs rather than solely on grading and ranking students. The following are examples of what various educators can do to implement this critical recommendation.

1. *Social studies supervisors and staff development specialists* can plan inservice programs designed to teach social studies teachers how to develop items and evaluation strategies that assess critical thinking skills and conceptual understanding and other areas not assessed by most teacher-made and many standardized tests. Social studies supervisors can work with evaluation consultants and teachers to develop a pool of test items that measure critical thinking skills and conceptual understanding in various social studies courses. Those items need to be keyed to the social studies objectives, weighted for difficulty, and shared with teachers throughout the district. Data from these items can be used for both program and student evaluation. Data on student attitudes and values can be used for program assessment but should not be used for grading students.

2. *Social studies district supervisors, chairpersons, and teachers* can take steps to include social studies in district accountability efforts. A variety of evaluative data should be used to determine the quality of district social studies programs, including student test results, attitude surveys, classroom observation, content analysis of texts, and ratings of learning activities by panels of educators. Any minimum competency tests used in social studies need to reflect the full range of social studies skills and understandings. Emphasis on some at the expense of others will eventually distort social studies programs by forcing concentration on those areas covered in the test.

3. *Social studies teachers* can make a committed effort to use tests that include the measurement of critical thinking, conceptual understanding, learning skills, and participatory skills. They can also share the tests they have developed and information about tests they have used with other teachers teaching the same course.

The Curriculum

Desired State

The social studies curriculum enables students to understand and function in the real world. Each school's curriculum is based on attention to the agreed-upon major goals and dimensions of social studies, and each promotes a nonrepetitive pattern of topics and courses and appropriate materials and activities. Local needs and resources are considered as individual curricula are developed, and congruence exists between each school's stated social studies curriculum and its actual practice.

Recommendations

A. Project SPAN recommends that social studies educators give renewed attention to reviewing, revising, and stating their views on the basic purpose and goals of social studies, taking into account all elements described in the SPAN curriculum desired state.

If effective participation in the social world is taken as the basic purpose of social studies, and knowledge, skills, values, and participation are accepted as the major goals, then it is imperative for social studies educators to elaborate these ideas and to think through the ways in which this purpose and these goals can each have substantial representation in the K–12 curriculum. It is also important for curriculum planners to arrive at a well thought out rationale for the emphasis to be given to each of the four goals and the various dimensions of a comprehensive social studies curriculum.

The starting point for rational and effective curriculum planning is consideration of the ultimate or basic purpose and goals to be achieved. The SPAN desired state for the curriculum presents a useful and defensible place to begin such work. However, even if other educators disagree with this view of the purpose and goals of social studies, the obligation remains to clarify whatever rationale, goals, and objectives they have for social studies. This phase of curriculum planning often gets short shrift in the hustle of curriculum planning and materials adoption. Rationales, goals, and objectives are not items to include in the beginning of curriculum guides and textbooks merely to satisfy a public-relations function. They must be considered and reconsidered as teachers, supervisors, and developers move through the process of determining the content, materials, learning activities, and evaluation procedures for their social studies programs. More time and thought devoted to purpose and goals at all levels of curriculum planning and implementation can lead to a more integrated and effective program.

1. *District social studies consultants and curriculum committees* can formulate statements of their district's commitment to the basic purpose and goals of social studies. Through publications, committees, and workshops, they can secure involvement in and commitment to the district's position on the basic purpose and goals of their social studies program.

2. *Social studies teachers* can clarify and state their views of the basic purpose and major goals of social studies and participate in school and districtwide efforts to review the rationale, goals, and objectives of their social studies program.

B. Project SPAN recommends that social studies educators at all levels examine their existing K–12 curricula, including their scopes and sequences and curriculum materials, to determine the extent to which they are consistent with the basic purpose and major goals of social studies, giving substantial attention to all the important elements of a comprehensive social studies curriculum.

It is not uncommon for elements of a curriculum to have little relationship to each other. Rationales, when they exist, may be so vague and general as to support any curiculum. Goals and objectives are often so broad and extensive as to give little guidance to the actual curriculum. The curriculum structure, in the form of a scope and sequence and/or a list of courses and topics, may be written by an *ad hoc* committee, put on the shelf, and forgotten. Curriculum materials, usually textbooks conforming to a national pattern, may have a limited relationship to locally-chosen goals and objectives; as a consequence, what is taught in the classroom, following the text, may have a limited relationship with local goals and objectives. Finally, evaluation methods, based on standardized tests or on teacher-made tests primarily related to the textbooks, may have little relationship to the stated rationale, goals, and objectives of the school or district.

Concerted efforts need to be made, therefore, to see that the rationale, goals, and objectives clarified by social studies educators are indeed reflected in the actual content, materials, and activities of their social studies programs. The first step in this process is to examine existing curricula to determine the extent to which they (a) deal with the four goals of knowledge, skills, values, and participation; (b) are based on the needs and abilities of students and the concerns of society as well as the nature of the disciplines; (c) focus on past, present, and future perspectives; and (d) include individual, societal, and global aspects. The following are some suggested activities that various social studies educators can undertake to help implement this objective.

1. *Social studies teachers* can examine their individual social studies courses, materials, and evaluation procedures to determine the degree to which they contribute to achievement of the basic purpose and goals and include all the important elements of a comprehensive social studies program. They can make their views known in the planning and revision of school and district curricula and selection of materials.

2. *District social studies supervisors and teachers,* through planning committees, can examine their district's K–12 social studies program to determine the extent to which it contributes to the basic purpose and goals of social studies. Included in the examination can be the district's social studies rationale, goals, objectives, materials, activities, and evaluation procedures. Strategies for redressing shortcomings and imbalances can be determined and implemented.

3. *District administrators and boards of education* can provide professional and financial support for the efforts of district teachers and consultants to define, revise, and implement social studies programs that are consonant with the basic purpose and goals of social studies.

C. Project SPAN recommends that support be given at all levels to the production of curriculum materials and teacher resources needed to address relatively neglected areas of the social studies curriculum, such as critical thinking, social participation, societal issues, and student developmental needs.

1. *Social studies consultants and district administrators* can support district efforts to produce curriculum materials that meet the basic purpose and goals of social studies and, at the same time, reflect local needs related to those goals and local resources that can contribute to them.

2. *Social studies teachers* can take individual responsibility for developing supplementary materials for at least one new unit of study per year, units that are not likely to be available from commercial publishers. Examples of subject matter for such units include local public issues, the local school culture, and local resource persons.

3. *State and district consultants and administrators* can use their pivotal positions as links between publishers and teachers to create awareness of the need for materials that genuinely support the basic purpose and goals of the district's social studies programs. Particularly in larger states and cities, they can work with publishers on the joint development of experimental innovative materials, with at least tentative assurance of adoption and use by the cooperating states or cities. Some such effort is essential to breaking the impasse created by the reasonable reluctance of publishers to put substantial resources into innovative materials and the reluctance of districts to plan innovative curricula for which suitable materials are available.

The Social Studies Profession

Desired State

All members of the profession have a common commitment to social studies education and work toward its improvement. They share a unity of purpose and belief in major goals, although diverse views on how to accomplish these goals are welcomed, given fair hearing, and reflected in practice. Working together, members of the profession maintain high standards of performance, press for professional growth, and welcome opportunities for a wide range of interactions.

Recommendations

A. Project SPAN recommends that social studies professionals engage in nation-wide debate and dialogue about the basic purpose and directions of social studies. The aim of the dialogue is to create one or a small number of statements about the rationale, goals, and objectives of social studies that will provide a sense of unity and direction for the profession.

Social studies can suffer from too much or too little focus. An authoritative, monolithic statement about the nature and purposes of social studies can discourage creative diversity, dissent, and change, just as excessive fragmentation of purposes can result in a destructive lack of unity and direction. What is needed is diversity within unity, flexibility within stability. In the late 1970s and early 80s, many felt a lack of unity and direction; movement toward a greater sense of unity may well be in order, but not at the expense of continued openness to change. Debate and discussion about these matters must involve all segments of the profession, not merely the academic scholars at universities. Examples of actions that may be taken by various groups to foster creative debate about social studies purposes follow.

1. *District administrators and school boards* can give administrative and financial support to participation on the part of their social studies professionals in this continuing, nationwide dialogue.

2. *District social studies consultants* can contribute to the nationwide dialogue by making available, through professional journals and meetings, the work of their local districts on rationales, goals and objectives, course content, activities, and evaluation procedures.

3. *Social studies teachers* can participate in the dialogue by extending their own professional reading, participating in inservice activities directed toward these goals, contributing to local, regional, and national journals, and participating in regional and national meetings focused on the purpose of social studies.

B. Project SPAN recommends that social studies professionals and other educators strive to create settings that foster constructive and cooperative work among social studies educators, other educators, and lay persons.

Social studies professionals can profit from greater communication among themselves, receiving support, ideas, and challenges from each other. They can profit from interactions with other educational professionals and lay persons by getting increased understanding and support from those persons and by responding to the criticisms and constructive suggestions of "outsiders." Outsiders, in turn, can profit by getting a better understanding of the goals and methods of the social studies educators and by having the opportunity to influence social studies programs.

Constructive and cooperative work among various groups and individuals can occur only if there is a will to work together, useful work to accomplish, and appropriate circumstances in which that work can be accomplished. Appropriate circumstances must be arranged, with attention to considerations such as appropriate meeting times and places, availability of participants, and availability of the required resources. Activities must be planned with clear statements of goals, agendas, and responsibilities and carried out with appropriate leadership, reports, and follow-up. Examples of actions that can be taken to foster such cooperative activities follow.

1. *Social studies teachers* can be brought together periodically for such purposes as updating content, improving instructional methods, and promoting professional development and involvement. Teachers, consultants, and administrators can share responsibility for planning and executing such meetings. At the secondary level, meetings can also be held with teachers of other subjects to promote cooperative efforts bridging different subjects. At the elementary level, some of the meetings can focus on ways in which teachers relate social studies to other subjects.

2. *District administrators and school boards* can give administrative and financial support to form and maintain districtwide social studies planning committees. Such planning committees, constituted of overlapping, rotating memberships, can have responsibility for monitoring new developments outside and inside the district, disseminating information, planning inservice activities with consultants and administrators, recommending curriculum materials, and designing evaluation procedures.

3. *State social studies consultants* can work with district consultants and social studies committees to plan statewide professional activities, including information dissemination, inservice programs, and other professional development activities. They can also work with regional and state accrediting agencies to ensure that accreditation documents and practices encourage and support appropriate professional standards and practices.

C. Project SPAN recommends that administrators and teachers recognize, encourage, and utilize the diversity and individuality that exists within the profession.

Students, teachers, administrators, consultants, and all other participants in educational endeavors have different goals, talents, and capacities. It is futile to expect uniformity in capabilities and performance, and it would be unfortunate if uniformity could be achieved. Diversity and individuality can enrich every educational endeavor; they are sources of new ideas and challenges to old ideas.

1. *Teachers* can take the initiative in determining what renewal opportunities and experiences are most suitable for their own continuing development. Each teacher can be prepared to submit periodically an individualized plan for updating and renewing his or her own professional development and improvement of teaching. In addition to recognizing and planning for their own professional growth, teachers can seek to encourage and capitalize on the differing talents and interests of their students. To the extent of their abilities, teachers can use a variety of teaching materials and learning experiences.

2. *Building principals and social studies consultants* can consider the individual characteristics and needs of their social studies teachers in planning and providing opportunities for professional growth and renewal. Administrative and financial support can be provided to assist the individualized professional development plans of teachers.

3. *All social studies educators* can provide platforms and sympathetic ears for the expression of diverse opinions, as well as reasonable latitude for a variety of approaches to social studies education. Persons with the power and influence to encourage or suppress diversity include planners of inservice programs and of local, regional, and national conferences; curriculum developers; teacher educators at universities; groups of parents and lay persons; and editors and publishers.

D. Project SPAN recommends that social studies educators promote and support a series of role exchanges to improve communication and understanding among members of the profession.

Role exchanges can greatly enhance personal effectiveness and broaden one's vision of the field of social studies and of education. Role exchange can increase communication, thus giving a better perspective on one's own problems and the problems of others, while introducing new ideas and techniques gleaned from peers in an action setting. Role exchanges can have the additional, incidental benefit of bringing variety to teacher and students.

1. *Social studies teachers* can exchange responsibilities, both with each other and with teachers of other subjects, providing a broader perspective on other teachers' curricula, students, and school cultures. Such exchanges can profitably take place between teachers in the same school, teachers in different schools, and teachers at different grade levels, including exchanges between teachers in magnet schools and feeder schools.

2. *Social studies consultants, administrators, and classroom teachers,* within and between districts, can exchange responsibilities, preferably for lengths of time sufficient to permit acquaintance with students and school personnel in the new settings. Such exchanges can help consultants and administrators keep in touch with changing student attitudes and behavior, with the classroom effectiveness of particular curriculum materials, and with a variety of problems seen from the viewpoint of the

classroom. The classroom teacher can get a better perspective on the responsibilities and problems of consultants and administrators.

Public Support

Desired State

School boards, parents, citizen groups, and the general public actively support social studies programs. Social studies teachers and supervisors are engaged in efforts to inform and involve the public. Most members of the public realize that many aspects of social studies lead to debates that contribute to the growth of good minds. They support efforts to present all sides of controversial issues, both in the schools and in public forums.

Recommendations

A. Project SPAN recommends that social studies educators conduct systematic efforts to demonstrate the nature and importance of social studies to the public.

One of the failures of the "new social studies" efforts of the 1960s and early 1970s was that their proponents tended to ignore the public until a crisis occurred. Social studies educators in the 1980s cannot afford to ignore the public. They must assume the initiative in convincing school boards, parent organizations, community groups, and other segments of the general public that social studies must be an integral part of a K–12 education. This involves explaining and illustrating what a good, comprehensive social studies program is and why it is important. Leadership in these efforts can be assumed at the national and state levels, but must be directly communicated at the local levels as well. The following actions can be taken by various groups in this effort.

1. *Social studies supervisors,* in conjunction with teachers and state and local social studies councils, can use this booklet and materials from their local programs to conduct awareness programs for parents and members of their communities. These sessions can also include the demonstration of activities that illustrate what social studies is and why it is important, as well as the presentation and discussion of materials. Special emphasis can be given to the importance of social studies at the elementary level.

2. *Social studies teachers* can take advantage of back-to-school programs and parent-teacher conferences to show parents what they are doing in social studies and why it is important. Teachers can emphasize to parents that social studies is more than memorizing facts from history and geography, that it includes understanding big ideas, learning thinking skills, and participating in the social world.

B. Project SPAN recommends that social studies educators actively involve members of the public in their social studies programs.

Involving community members and the public in social studies programs can help to bring the real social world closer to the students. It can also help to increase public understanding of social studies and its importance in young people's education and thus increase public support for social studies. Recent experience in many states with law-related education is illustrative. Lawyers, judges, police, and other community members have demonstrated considerable support for law-related education and social studies programs as a result of their extensive involvement in these programs. These efforts should be broadened to include many other members of the public in other aspects of social studies programs. The following actions illustrate some things social studies educators can do to encourage this involvement.

1. *Social studies teachers* can include and involve members of their communities in their social studies programs in a variety of ways. Parents can be used to help on field trips and to offer places where students can conduct community learning activities. Many different members of the community can also be effective guest speakers for social studies classes—including lawyers, judges, political officials, social scientists, and businesspersons.

2. *Social studies supervisors* can coordinate efforts to establish a file of resource people from the community who can serve as guest speakers or hosts for community learning activities for social studies programs.

3. *Social studies supervisors* and other administrators can involve members of the community, through the school board and parent organizations, in the process of curriculum revision and materials selection. The nature of this participation can range from reactions to drafts or preliminary plans to formal membership on committees.

Part Four

An Alternative Approach

Chapter Ten

Social Roles: A Focus for Social Studies in the 1980s

Douglas P. Superka
Sharryl Davis Hawke

SPAN HAS OUTLINED SIX MAJOR PROBLEMS that social studies educators need to address in the 1980s and a series of desired states and recommendations for improving social studies. Since those statements are broad guidelines, a number of different approaches to social studies could be advocated to implement the recommendations and achieve the desired states. This section offers one such approach.

Seven Social Roles

How can social studies contribute more fully to the development of knowledgeable and effective participants in our society? One way would be to focus content and instruction more directly on how most people participate in society—how they spend their time and where they put their energy. Most people's social lives can be described by seven major roles: citizen, worker, consumer, family member, friend, member of various social groups, and self. Social studies can help young people understand, value, and function creatively and competently in these social roles—thereby helping them become effective individuals and effective participants in our society.

The term "role" has been defined by sociologists and psychologists in various ways. There is general agreement that the term refers to a set of organized meanings and values that direct a person's actions in a given situation or in the performance of a given function (Kitchens and Muessig, 1980; Rose, 1965). Most anthropologists and sociologists add that these roles are usually ascribed to people by their society or culture. Some emphasize the interactive nature of this process and that individuals still can exercise choice in defining and implementing their roles (e.g. Blumer, 1970). The term role is used here in roughly this manner. Particular attention is directed to situations (especially sets of relationships) and functions implied by a role.

Each of the seven roles defines an important area of social life in which nearly all persons participate and each implies a specific set of relationships and functions. While each role defines a distinct set of relationships and functions, all seven roles are interrelated. Social studies programs can highlight both the distinctiveness of and the interrelationships among the seven social roles.

The idea of a social roles focus is not completely new in education, although these seven roles are somewhat different from previous formulations. A similar theme can be found in the "seven cardinal principles" of the 1918 NEA report, which included worthy home membership, vocation, citizenship, worthy use of leisure, and ethical character (Commission on the Reorganization of Secondary Education, 1918). More recently, two social studies educators have proposed an emphasis on "lifelong roles"—citizenship, family membership, occupation, avocation, and personal efficacy—for elementary social studies (Joyce and Alleman-Brooks, 1979).

Citizen

Citizenship education has been considered the central goal of social studies for at least the last century (Hertzberg, 1981). Moreover, within the context of the recent resurgence of interest in the topic, citizenship has been called the "primary, overriding purpose" (Barr and others, 1977), the "centering concept" (Shaver, 1977), and the "ultimate justification" (Remy, 1978b) of social studies. The revised NCSS curriculum guidelines, state frameworks, district curriculum guides, and textbooks reflect this orientation.

Despite widespread agreement about its centrality and importance to social studies, however, there is little agreement about the meaning of citizenship, the nature and scope of the citizen role, or the major focus of citizenship education efforts (Meyer, 1979). While some educators have stressed patriotism and loyalty, others have emphasized problem solving and social criticism. Some definitions of citizenship encompass nearly all areas of social life, while others are restricted to the political arena. Nearly everyone, however, agrees that the development of responsible participating citizens is a key to preserving and improving our democratic society.

Our definition of the citizen role focuses on the relationships between individuals and political entities (for example, the state, governmental agencies, and political organizations) and organized efforts to influence public policy. On the basis of this conception, the citizen role includes a wide range of important activities: voting, obeying just laws, challenging unjust laws, paying taxes, serving in the armed forces, participating in political parties, studying public issues, advocating positions on public policy questions (either individually or in groups), working for volunteer organizations, and holding public office. Citizens engage in these activities in a variety of settings and at several levels, including the neighborhood, community, city, state, region, nation, and world, with the specific nature of the citizen activities differing at the different levels. Many of the activities performed at the city, state, and national levels are directly related to government institutions, while those at the neighborhood, region, and world levels are not.

In relation to all levels of the citizen role, social studies has a major and unique contribution to make. Although other subject areas and aspects of school share some responsibility for citizen education, social studies is primarily responsible for providing opportunity for students to learn the basic knowledge, skills, and values needed to understand and participate effectively in the United States political system and to analyze and help resolve public issues.

Worker

The worker role, unlike the citizen role, is not generally perceived by social studies educators as being central to their field. Although some educators have supported the "infusion" of career awareness into social studies instruction (e.g. Taylor and others, 1977; National Council for the Social Studies, 1975), many teachers have viewed career education as an encroachment on the legitimate domain of social studies.

Social studies educators cannot ignore the fact that productive work is one of the most important aspects of most people's lives. A consistent finding of the various secondary education commissions of the 1970s was that education had failed to establish a meaningful relationship between school and work in our society (National Task Force for High School Reform, 1975; National Commission on the Reform of Secondary Education, 1973; Panel on Youth, 1974).

What can social studies contribute to this role? Its responsibility in this area is auxiliary, not primary. The major responsibility must and should rest with career education specialists, guidance counselors, and language arts and mathematics teachers. Social studies can reinforce these efforts. Social studies also shares with other areas of school and society some responsibility for developing decision-making skills and constructive attitudes toward work.

In addition to these shared responsibilities, social studies has the following special functions: to provide students with awareness of careers directly related to the social sciences (for example, urban planner, sociologist, government administrator, and business economist); to help students reflect on their worker-related experiences (such as analyzing interpersonal relationships and conflicts on the job); to provide students with knowledge that will place in historical and social perspective the role of the worker in U.S. society and the world (knowledge about labor unions, immigration and employment, women in the labor force, and the impact of war on jobs); and to help students analyze and discuss the interrelationships between the worker role and the other social roles (the conflicts that often arise between being a responsible member of the family and a conscientious worker).

Consumer

While not all people are workers or active citizens, everyone in our society is a consumer. The role of consumer is to buy and use the goods and services produced by workers. These goods and services include natural resources (water, wood, oil, and gas), manufactured products (food, drugs, bicycles, and cars), information (print and other media), business services (banking, insurance, and real estate), and social services (education, medicine, recreation, and welfare). The consumer role includes being a good planner, shopper, and protector of these goods and services and an effective money manager. Being a wise and competent consumer in our modern complex society will continue to be a major challenge in the 1980s and beyond.

The consumer role is sometimes perceived as an economic activity in which persons engage solely for their own individual benefit. The problems related to using energy and other environmental resources have demonstrated that the consumer role also has significant collective and societal dimensions. Buying a small car instead of a large one, for example, may be a long-term money saver for an individual. It may also be a more environmentally sound and socially responsible decision.

Social studies' major contribution to the role of consumer can be to help students understand this role in the context of our national economic, political, and social systems and to appreciate the global interdependence of consumers. Meeting these goals for consumer-role education suggests such topics as consumer law, supply and demand, consumer protection, inflation, money and credit, boycotts, energy, the environment, multinational corporations, and international trade. It also calls for teaching about interrelationships between the consumer and the other social roles.

Family Member

Most demographers predict that the 1980s will not be an easy, stable time for families in the United States. Divorce rates will probably continue to rise, birth rates will remain low, more women will join the paid labor force, more children will live with only one parent, and more couples will decide not to have children. Despite these stresses, strains, and changes, most experts believe that the American family will adapt and survive. Because of these stresses, strains, and changes, young people will need all the help they can get to understand and function in their roles as family members.

Family roles include mother, father, husband, wife, son, daughter, brother, and sister; also grandchild, grandparent, mother-in-law, and still others. Everyone functions in two or more family roles, often in two or more simultaneously. The nature of each of these roles changes dramatically over the course of a person's life. Societal trends add another element of change.

Social studies programs can and should make an important contribution to helping young people understand and function in their present and future roles as family members. Obviously, social studies cannot and should not be totally responsible for producing "good family members"; a young person's own family will certainly be the major influence. However, by drawing on knowledge from sociology, psychology, anthropology, and history, social studies can help students better understand and deal with parent-child relationships, sibling relationships, the rights and responsibilities of parents and children, changing family roles, the family as an institution, the future of the family, the diverse types of families in the United States and throughout the world, and marriage and courtship.

At present, the family is a specific focus of social studies only in the primary grades (especially grade 1) and in the 12th grade, as part of a sociology or family life elective; in other grades it is virtually ignored, despite the importance of family to the lives of early adolescents. The role of family member should have a more prominent place in K–12 social studies programs.

Friend

No social studies teacher, especially at the junior and senior high levels, has to be reminded that friends are one of the most important dimensions of students' lives. A recent study of teenage sexuality confirmed the importance of friendships in the lives of 15- to 18-year-olds ("Sex Rated Below Friends, School, and Sports," 1979). Younger students also value friendship, but they think about it differently. According to research conducted by Robert Selman and Anne Selman (1979) children's thinking about friendship develops in stages in much the same way as their reasoning about moral issues and other interpersonal relationships. The Selmans also found that many youngsters need help in making and keeping friends and in dealing with friendship-related conflicts.

The importance of friends does not appear to diminish as one grows into adulthood, although the nature, forms, and bases of friendship change dramatically. While we lack extensive research data on friendships, such popular-culture indices as television shows ("Laverne and Shirley") and singles-club memberships suggest the importance of friendship in our society. The few studies that do exist (Block, 1980, and Parlee, 1979) confirm that the experience of friendship is crucial to the healthy social and emotional development of children and adults. Strained family relationships and alienation from the community underline the importance of friends as a source of trust, understanding, affection, and acceptance.

In contrast to the centrality of friendship in people's lives, the topic is virtually nonexistent in social studies. A few primary-level textbooks touch on the subject and some supplementary materials contain activities related to friendship. Of all the social roles, however, that of friend receives by far the least emphasis in social studies.

Social studies (along with language arts and counseling) has an important and legitimate contribution to make in this area. While a new educational movement is not being suggested here, there are some vital aspects of friendship that can be a part of schooling and social studies. Many students at all levels will respond to opportunities to examine and discuss questions related to friendship, and the social sciences have important knowledge and skills to offer in educating students for the role of friend. Appropriate topics include forms of friendship, ranging from casual to intimate, responsibilities and expectations associated with friendship, qualities of good friends, processes of making friends, social mobility, same-sex/opposite-sex friendships, conflicts between family and friends, peer groups, cross-culture friendships, and wartime friendships.

Member of Social Groups

In addition to functioning in the other social roles, every person is also a member of various social groups. Broadly defined, these include (1) groups whose membership is determined at birth (being male or female, a member of a racial group, and a member of an age cohort group); (2) such categories as religious groups, ethnic groups, and socioeconomic classes into which persons are born but from which they may move; and (3) groups to which people choose to belong, such as bridge clubs, baseball teams, and consciousness-raising groups.

Participation and membership in all these groups can take place at various levels of involvement; however, certain socially-prescribed expectations and norms are associated with membership in each group. Social studies efforts in regard to membership in the first two kinds of groups should be focused on teaching students to be aware of the existence and nature of different kinds of groups, to analyze their particular affiliations with groups, to make conscious individual decisions about the extent of their participation in various groups, and to understand the nature and origins of group expectations—emphasizing that one does not necessarily have to limit one's choices because of traditional group expectations. This has indeed been a major thrust of many multicultural education, ethnic studies, and women's equity efforts.

At the most intimate level, a person can choose to belong to a small face-to-face group whose primary goal is social or philosophical rather than political or whose organizing principle may be ethnic identity, religion, age, or sex. Some examples of groups in this category would be a social club based mainly on ethnic affiliation, a youth athletic club, a bridge club, and a local church or temple.

At still another level, a social group may be a large-scale (national or global) organization whose purpose is to help maintain and improve the social conditions of a particular group—for example, the National Organization for Women (NOW) and the National Association for the Advancement of Colored People (NAACP). The role of social studies in regard to such a group is to teach about its nature, purpose, function, and impact and to help students make reflective decisions about possible participation.

Still another type of group is a social aggregate lacking any kind of formal organization—males in the United States, children in the world, and Jews, for example. This category also includes members of geographically defined aggregates: people who live in the same river valley, mountain range, or desert, who have no political organization but share certain values and behavior because of their interaction with a common environment. Here the major role of social studies is to teach about the impact and contributions of such groups in the United States and the world—with attention to the groups' cultural traditions, customs, and history, and the effects of major historical or contemporary forces on their social welfare.

Social studies can contribute to students' understanding of the group-member role by focusing on the interrelationships between this role and the other social roles. Family roles, for example, are closely related to membership in ethnic groups. Another crucial topic is the potential conflict between the citizen role and membership in these social groups. Recent multicultural education efforts have helped to emphasize the pluralistic nature of our society and therefore of citizenship in the United States. Some, however, view this as fragmentation of the society and subordination of national civic values to ethnic and cultural values. The possible interrelationships between the citizen role and religious group member role have been dramatized by the direct involvement of some religious groups in recent political campaigns. Teaching directly and honestly about these kinds of conflicts and interrelationships today and in the past is a significant responsibility of social studies.

Self

United States society expects a person to be a good citizen, worker, consumer, family member, and to a lesser extent a good friend. In addition, our society often conveys certain expected ways a person should act based on one's sex, ethnic group, and social class. There is still another expectation our society places on people, because of the high value it puts on the individual: people are also encouraged to be themselves—to express their own uniqueness and to develop their full potentialities. This striving for fulfillment and realization as a unique and competent person occurs both within the six social roles (for example, by being a unique teacher or the best father you can possibly be) and outside those roles (by reading history to expand one's intellectual horizons or running ten miles a day to develop and maintain a healthy body). We have defined this function and the sets of relationships, meanings, and values associated with it as the role of self.[1]

The importance of including a focus on self has been recognized by many educators within and outside the social studies field. Goals of increasing self-awareness and enhancing self-esteem have been a central aspect of humanistic education and values clarification (e.g., Canfield and Wells, 1976; Raths and others, 1978). Many social studies educators also include these goals (e.g., Fenton, 1977).

As in the other roles, the role of self involves the person in certain kinds of activities. In addition to acting competently in the other roles, these self-development-oriented activities include developing a positive and realistic self-concept, increasing one's self-awareness, expanding one's intellectual capacities, developing and maintaining a healthy emotional and physical being, and clarifying and living by a set of personal values that leads to individual and societal well-being.

All aspects of school and society share some responsibility for education and development related to the role of self. What is the unique contribution of social studies to this goal? It consists primarily of providing learning experiences that will help students understand how the other social roles, including membership in social groups, influence identity and self-development, as well as how the latter can influence and change social roles. To accomplish this goal social studies can draw on the social sciences—from psychology, sociology, social psychology, history, anthropology, and cultural geography—as well as on sources such as multicultural education, sex-role awareness, literature, and philosophy.

Why Social Roles?

The goal of refocusing social studies on social roles cannot be easily attained, nor will it be a magical panacea for the problems of social studies. The social roles focus is recommended in the belief that it will help, more than some existing approaches, to alleviate the six problems described by Project SPAN and move social studies toward the desired states. The effect of social roles on four of the six problems is discussed here.

---

[1]While it may not be common to use the term "self" as a "role" as it is used here, we believe this is convenient terminology for our present purpose, emphasizing the important relationship of the self to the "other" six social roles. This usage is similar to that of some sociologists and philosophers who have focused on an interactionist perspective on self and society (e.g., Bigge, 1971; Blumer, 1970). A similar view of the self role has also been taken by some social studies educators (e.g., Haas, 1981).

Student Learning

The most important problem to be addressed in the 1980s, and by implication the ultimate desired state to be achieved, is related to student learning and valuing of social studies. Since social roles focus on how children and adults really spend time and act in the social world, this orientation should help students appreciate the importance of social studies, increase student motivation to learn social studies, and, ultimately, improve students' learning of significant knowledge and skills in social studies.

The social roles focus can help students see the value of social studies. Can it also lead to increased learning of important social studies knowledge and skills? A case can be made for social roles having more potential to do that than some other approaches. First, the social roles provide a framework for asking: What knowledge and skills are most important for living in the social world? If helping students become effective participants in the social world is the ultimate goal of social studies, the social roles focus might lead to a clarification of knowledge and skills that are more directly related to that goal and not entirely different from the knowledge and skills now being taught.

Second, social roles is more likely than other approaches to improve student learning, because it has a greater potential for stimulating student interest and motivation. A recent meta-analysis of education research has demonstrated a consistent and positive relationship between student motivation and attitudes and student learning (Walberg and others, 1979). Common sense also suggests that students learn more when they are interested and involved in a subject and when they believe it is important and useful to them.

Third, a social roles framework has a great potential to incorporate and use the knowledge about student cognitive, moral, and social development that has been gained in the past decade or two. Unlike approaches that focus on one aspect of social studies (such as influencing public policy, learning the basic facts and generalizations of the discipline, or being a responsible citizen), the social roles approach with its balanced emphasis on personal, interpersonal, and societal issues will lend itself readily to integrating the implications of a wide range of child development research.

Suggesting the potential for social roles to use knowledge of student needs and interest is not to advocate a total focus on student interest. Some structure, such as that of the social roles, is needed to provide a stable focus within which student concerns can be considered, without creating a curriculum that is repetitious or unduly concentrated on the egocentric orientations of students.

Curriculum

The major problem with the social studies curriculum today, as identified by Project SPAN, is that it is not organized around or focused on personal and societal goals that help students become effective participants in the social world. The social roles focus is designed to alleviate this problem by emphasizing the wide range of roles in which people engage—from mainly personal ones such as friend and family member to societal ones such as consumer and citizen. The social roles framework, moreover, provides an excellent way to integrate the many diverse topic areas such as legal education, multicultural studies, consumer education, and career education. The roles also provide an understandable framework for integrating knowledge from history and the social science disciplines and for explicating the major knowledge, skill, value, and participation goals of social studies.

The roles have strong potential for developing a comprehensive social studies curriculum based on personal and societal issues. Moreover, the roles provide a curriculum focus that can integrate three previously competing perspectives of social studies—subject, learner, and society.

Profession

One of the primary needs identified by Project SPAN for improving the profession is to develop a greater unity of purpose and direction for social studies instruction. In the last 20 years a number of approaches and rationales for social studies have been posited, including reflective inquiry, social science disciplines, citizenship transmission, and student-centered (Morrissett and Haas, 1982). The critical need now is to develop approaches to social studies that synthesize the best elements of each of these various perspectives and point toward helping students understand and act effectively in their social lives.

One such approach is the roles focus, which calls for providing learning experiences and for teaching knowledge, skills, and values that will help students understand and act effectively in the major roles in which they engage in the social world. This will require students to learn facts, concepts, and generalizations from history and the social science disciplines; it will involve developing reflective thinking and rational decision-making skills; and it will include developing some basic values and discussing value issues. But instead of doing these things for their own sake and instead of competing for attention, proponents of these approaches can see where and how each of their views fits into the overall purpose of social studies. The roles, therefore, can be an effective way to provide a greater sense of unity and direction to the profession.

Moreover, efforts to establish a social roles focus on a K-12 basis can encourage interaction among elementary, junior high, and senior high social studies teachers. This would, of course, be true for any attempt to provide a K-12 focus for social studies, but the social roles, more than other approaches to social studies, also provides a strong basis for fostering communication between social studies educators and other subject area teachers.

Finally, the roles focus can contribute to alleviating teacher dissatisfaction by providing teachers with a comprehensive and understandable statement of the central purpose of social studies—a purpose that can also be understood and supported by students. In addition, social roles provides a framework whereby teachers of all grade levels and of varying perspectives can contribute to achieving this purpose.

Public Awareness

The sixth problem identified by Project SPAN points to the need for more public awareness of, support for, and involvement in social studies in the 1980s. This will not be easily attained. The adult public, according to a recent Gallup poll (1978), shares the students' belief that their social studies classes were not very useful and relevant to their lives. Paradoxically, they still rate U.S. history and government as essential subjects (Gallup, 1979). Both views, however, are probably tied to the realities they experienced as students—those courses were required for them and they were not very relevant to them. Personal and societal relevancy is one important aspect of the social roles approach. If social studies educators can demonstrate this to the public, a major step toward public understanding and support can be achieved.

Thus, efforts to educate the public must occur when we try to gain involvement and support. The social roles have an important advantage over other social studies reform approaches in these efforts. The roles can be explained in simple, understandable terms—citizen, consumer, worker, friend, parent, child, and so on—to which the public can relate. Previous reform approaches had to overcome jargonistic terms such as "interdisciplinary social science concepts" and "reflective inquiry processes" when communicating with lay people.

Some Questions About Social Roles

Would adoption of social roles as an organizing focus mean virtual abandonment of the present social studies curriculum?

No; much of the present content could be kept. Many existing courses, current activities, and available materials contain valuable elements for teaching social roles. Historical perspectives and concepts, for example, are valuable sources of knowledge to help people understand and function well as citizens, consumers, family members, and so on, in our rapidly changing society.

Would adoption of social roles as a focus of social studies relegate citizenship to a minor role in the curriculum?

No; citizenship could, and probably should, remain the single most important role in social studies. Citizenship would, however, give way to greater emphasis on the other roles than currently exists.

In a curriculum based on social roles, is there any place for topics based on social concerns that have come into the curriculum recently—such as multicultural studies, women's studies, future studies, and global issues?

Yes; social roles can provide a useful framework for selecting and organizing subject matter related to these concerns. Studying families of different ethnic groups or in different cultures, for example, will not only enhance multicultural awareness but will help students place their own family roles and membership in ethnic groups in perspective. Focusing on the possible roles of consumers and workers in the 21st century can add additional relevance to future-studies programs.

Doesn't a focus on social roles imply that students are to be indoctrinated into passive acceptance of the roles assigned to them by society?

Like any other focus, the roles provide a setting within which students can and should deal with the interplay between individual goals and societal goals, social maintenance and social change, and self-actualization and socialization. Most of these social roles have changed dramatically in the last 20 years; more changes in the future are inevitable. Preparing students for these and other emerging roles in the future will mean much more than instilling a set of proper norms and behaviors.

Doesn't a social roles emphasis suggest a low level of intellectual endeavor—a "Mickey Mouse" type of curriculum?

As with any other goal or focus, it would be easy to reduce social roles to triviality—with courses such as "Your Friends in History" and "One Hundred Ways to Enhance Your Self-Concept Through Geography." This need not happen. The examples given in the preceding pages should indicate that it is possible to focus on social roles while maintaining the intellectual integrity of history and the social sciences.

Doesn't an emphasis on social roles in social studies imply that social studies will bear sole responsibility for developing informed, competent, and committed citizens, workers, consumers, and so on?

No; other subject areas and aspects of school life have important contributions to those roles. Science teachers, for example, share at least an equal responsibility with social studies teachers for helping students become wise consumers of energy and other environmental resources. Beyond the school, other social institutions (such as the family, media, business, and church) have a powerful influence in social roles development. A young person's own family, for instance, has an enormous impact on the kind of parent or spouse he or she will be. Social studies, however, does have a valuable contribution to make to education related to the social roles—within the school, probably the greatest contribution.

Conclusion

We have attempted to demonstrate how a social roles focus is consistent with Project SPAN's analysis of major problems and statements of desired states for social studies in the 1980s and may be more effective than some existing approaches in helping to achieve those desired states. We are not implying, however, that this focus is the only way or that it is a proven way to alleviate those problems and move toward those desired states. We welcome other viewpoints on how to accomplish those improvements. Meanwhile, we have submitted "social roles" as one specific suggestion for helping to make social studies more useful and worthwhile for elementary and secondary students in the 1980s and beyond.

Appendix
The National Science
Foundation Studies

THE INFORMATION IN THE PRECEDING CHAPTERS is based in part on the findings of three studies commissioned by the National Science Foundation. The following excerpts describing how those studies were conducted are from *The Status of Pre-College Science, Mathematics, and Social Studies Educational Practices in U.S. Schools: An Overview and Summaries of Three Studies* (SE-78-71).

1977 National Survey

The 1977 National Survey of Science, Mathematics, and Social Studies Education was conducted by the Research Triangle Institute.

The survey utilized a national probability sample of districts, schools, and teachers. The sample was designed so that every superintendent and principal, and every teacher and supervisor of science, mathematics, and social studies in grades K–12 in the United States had a chance of being selected. All public, Catholic, and private schools in the country were included in the target population.

The samples were selected using a multistage stratified cluster design. First, approximately 400 public school districts were selected from 102 different geographic areas across the country. Next, schools within these districts were selected to provide a total of approximately 400 schools at each of four grade levels: K–3, 4–6, 7–9, and 10–12. Finally, teachers within each sample school were selected from a list provided by the principal. Three teachers were selected from each K–3 and 4–6 sample school—one to answer questions about science instruction, one about mathematics instruction, and one about social studies instruction. Six teachers—two in each subject—were selected from each 7–9 and 10–12 sample school.

An initial review of the research literature was conducted to locate previous studies in science, mathematics, and social studies instruction and to identify important variables. A preliminary set of research questions and data sources was developed, submitted to NSF, and revised based on NSF feedback. Preliminary drafts of questionnaires were prepared with items that could be used to answer research questions.

The preliminary drafts of the questionnaires were reviewed by NSF and by 18 consultants with expertise in science, mathematics, and social studies education, and by representatives of a number of professional organizations.

After final revision and approval, the final versions of the questionnaires included the following topics:

State Supervisor: time spent on various supervision/coordination activities; sources of information; attendance at NSF-sponsored workshops; dissemination of federally-funded curriculum materials; requirements for high school graduation; and problems affecting instruction in their states.

District Curriculum Developers: job responsibilities; professional memberships and activities; sources of information; district guidelines; use of standardized tests; textbook selection; use of federally-funded curriculum materials; and problems affecting instruction in their districts.

Superintendents: background information such as district enrollment, type of community, per pupil expenditure, funding sources, number of teachers, and number of district supervisors; and opinions about federal support for curriculum development.

Principals: school enrollment, type of community; principal's qualifications for supervising science, mathematics, and social studies instruction; sources of information; attendance at NSF-sponsored activities; school facilities, equipment, and supplies; textbook selection; problems affecting instruction in their schools; use of federally-funded curriculum materials; and course offerings and enrollments in science, mathematics, and social studies.

Teachers: number of years teaching; sources of information; needs for assistance; time spent in instruction; teaching techniques; use of audiovisual materials; use of federally-funded curriculum materials; attendance at NSF-sponsored activities; and problems affecting instruction in their schools.

Questionnaires were mailed to teachers, principals, and local district supervisors. In districts with no district supervisor in one or more subject areas, the superintendent was asked to designate a person to answer questions about district programs.

Follow-up activities used to increase the response rates included thank-you/reminder postcards, a second questionnaire mail-out, mailgrams, and phone calls.

Completed questionnaires were edited manually and coded to resolve multiple responses and to assign numeric values to open-ended responses. The data were then transformed to machine-readable form using programmable terminals, and a number of machine-editing checks were performed. Responses that were outside the acceptable range were coded as "bad data" and excluded from the analyses.

The final step in file preparation was the addition of sampling weights to the file. The weight assigned to each sample member was the inverse of the probability of being selected into the sample; these weights were then adjusted for nonresponse of sample members. All results of the survey were calculated using weighted data.

These data, as in all surveys, were based on the self-report of respondents. In addition, the results of any sample survey, as opposed to a census of the entire population, were subject to sample variability. Results would not be exactly the same if a second random sample were drawn.

For a complete discussion of the results of the national survey, see Iris R. Weiss, *National Survey of Science, Mathematics, and Social Studies Education* (Washington, D.C.: National Science Foundation, 1978).

The Case Studies

Case Studies in Science Education is a collection of field observations of science teaching and learning in American public schools during the school year 1976–77. The study was organized by a team of education researchers at the University of Illinois.

Eleven high schools and their feeder schools were selected to provide a diverse and balanced group of sites: rural and urban; east, west, north and south; racially diverse; economically well-off and impoverished; constructing schools and closing schools; innovative and traditional. They were finally selected so that a researcher with ample relevant field experience could be placed at each. To confirm findings of the ethnographic case studies and to add special information, a national stratified random sample of about 4000 teachers, principals, curriculum supervisors, superintendents, parents, and senior class students were surveyed. Survey questions were based on observations at the 11 case-study sites.

The field researchers were instructed to find out what was happening and what people believed was important in science (including mathematics and social science) programs. On-site from four to 15 weeks, researchers were not required to coordinate their work with observers at other sites. Questions originally indicated important by the NSF or identified early in the field were "networked" by the Illinois team. Efforts to triangulate findings were assisted by reports of site visit teams.

Each observer prepared a case study report that was preserved intact as part of the final collection, and later augmented with cross-site conclusions by the Illinois team.

The case studies are described in full in Robert E. Stake and Jack A. Easley, Jr., *Case Studies in Science Education* (Washington, D.C.: National Science Foundation, 1978).

The Literature Review

The third study was a review and analysis of the literature related to the status of (1) existing practices in schools and in teacher education for the period 1955 through 1975, and (2) needs assessment efforts that have focused on local and national concerns. It was conducted by the Center for Science and Mathematics Education at The Ohio State University and the Social Science Education Consortium, Inc. An archival search of the literature was conducted using such data bases as ERIC, reports to federal educational agencies, *Dissertation Abstracts International, Education Index,* state department of education reports, summary data from governmental and professional studies, professional journals and scholarly works, summary data from various accrediting agencies, and other available documents.

The literature was searched and reviewed following parallel strategies for the two areas of practices and needs. Both descriptive literature on existing practices and the research/evaluation literature on effectiveness and efficiency of practices were included. Documents of particular significance were sought on completed needs assessment efforts to determine both goals and progress. The compiled literature was analyzed, evaluated, and summarized. These summaries are status reports of trends or patterns in the preparation of teachers, teaching practices, facilities, curriculum materials, achievement and attitudes of students, and needs expressed during the period as they were reflected in the literature.

A complete bibliography of the Social Studies/Social Science literature review is included in Karen B. Wiley, *The Status of Pre-College Science, Mathematics, and Social Science Education: 1955–1975, Volume III* (Washington D.C.: National Science Foundation, 1977).

Bibliography

Alexandria Public Schools. *Social Studies Curriculum, K–12*. Alexandria, Va., 1977.

Anderson, Lee, F., gen. ed. *Windows on Our World*. Boston: Houghton Mifflin, 1976.

Anderson, Lee. "Barriers to Change in Social Studies." In *The Current State of Social Studies: A Report of Project SPAN*. Boulder, Colo.: Social Science Education Consortium, 1982.

Armstrong, David G. *Social Studies in Secondary Education*. New York: Macmillan, 1980.

Barr, Robert D.; Barth, James L.; and Shermis, S. Samuel. *Defining the Social Studies*. Arlington, Va.: National Council for the Social Studies, 1977.

Barth, James L., and Shermis, S. Samuel. "Defining the Social Studies: An Exploration of Three Traditions." *Social Education* 34 (November 1970): 743–751.

Barth, James L., and Shermis, S. Samuel. "Social Studies Goals: The Historical Perspective." *Journal of Research and Development in Education* 13 (Winter 1980): 1–11.

Beard, Charles A. *A Charter for the Social Sciences in the Schools*. New York: Charles Scribner's Sons, 1932.

Berelson, Bernard. "Introduction." In *The Social Studies and the Social Sciences*. New York: Harcourt, Brace, and World, 1962.

Berman, Paul, and McLaughlin, Milbrey Wallin. *Federal Programs Supporting Educational Change. Vol. 8: Implementing and Sustaining Innovations*. Santa Monica: Rand Corporation, 1978.

Bigge, Morris L. *Positive Relativism: An Emergent Educational Philosophy*. New York: Harper and Row, 1971.

Block, Joel D. *Friendship*. New York: Macmillan, 1980.

Bloom, Benjamin S., ed. *Taxonomy of Educational Objectives: The Classification of Educational Goals. Handbook I: The Cognitive Domain*. New York: David McKay, 1956.

Blumer, Herbert. "Sociological Implications of the Thought of George Herbert Mead." In *Social Psychology Through Symbolic Interactionism*. Edited by G. P. Stone and H. A. Farberman. Waltham, Mass.: Ginn-Blaisdell, 1970.

Boulding, Kenneth E. *Ecodynamics: A New Theory of Societal Evolution*. Menlo Park, Calif.: Addison-Wesley, 1981.

Boulding, Kenneth; Kuhn, Alfred; and Senesh, Lawrence. *System Analysis and Its Use in the Classroom*. Boulder, Colo.: Social Science Education Consortium, 1973.

Boulding, Kenneth E.; Boulding, Elise; and Burgess, Guy. *The Social System of the Planet Earth*. Beverly Hills, Calif.: Sage, 1980.

Bowler, Mike. "Selling the 3 R's." (Six-part series.) *Baltimore Sun*, October 3–8, 1976.

Bowles, Samuel, and Gintis, Herbert. *Schooling in Capitalist America: Educational Reform and the Contradictions of Economic Life*. New York: Basic Books, 1976.

Bronfenbrenner, Urie. *The Ecology of Human Development: Experiments by Nature and Design*. Cambridge, Mass.: Harvard University Press, 1979.

Brophy, Jere, and Evertson, Carolyn. *Process-Product Correlations in the Texas Teacher Effectiveness Study: Final Report*. Austin: University of Texas Research and Development Center for Teacher Education, 1974.

Brubaker, Dale L. *Alternative Directions for the Social Studies*. Scranton, Penn.: International Textbook Co., 1967.

Brubaker, Dale L.; Simon, Lawrence H.; and Williams, Jo Watts. "A Conceptual Framework for Social Studies Curriculum and Instruction." *Social Education* 41 (1977): 201–205.

BSCS. *Biological Sciences Curriculum Study Journal* 2 (September 1979).

Buros, Oscar K., ed. *The Eighth Mental Measurements Yearbook*. Highland Park, N.J.: Gryphon Press, 1978.

Butts, R. Freeman. "The Revival of Civic Learning: A Rationale for the Education of Citizens." *Social Education* 43 (May 1979): 359–364.

Butts, R. Freeman. *The Revival of Civic Learning: A Rationale for Citizenship in American Schools*. Bloomington, Ind.: Phi Delta Kappa, 1980.

California Department of Education. *History-Social Science Framework for California Public Schools*. Preliminary edition. Sacramento: Department of Education, 1981.

Canfield, Jack, and Wells, Harold G. *100 Ways to Enhance Self-Concept*. Englewood Cliffs, N.J.: Prentice-Hall, 1976.

Carswell, Ronald J. B. "Evaluation of Affective Learning in Geographic Education." In *Evaluation in Geographic Education*. Edited by D. G. Kurfman. Belmont, Calif.: Fearon, 1970.

Cassidy, Edward W., and Kurfman, Dana G. "Decision Making as Purpose and Process." In *Developing Decision-Making Skills*. Edited by D. G. Kurfman. Arlington, Va.: National Council for the Social Studies, 1977.

Classroom Treatment of the Right to Work. Fairfax, Va.: National Right to Work Committee, 1978.

Cole, Sheila. "Send Our Children to Work?" *Psychology Today* 14 (July 1980): 44–68.

Coleman, James S., and others. *Youth: Transition to Adulthood*. Report of the Panel on Youth of the President's Science Advisory Committee. Chicago: University of Chicago Press, 1974.

College Entrance Examination Board. *About the Achievement Tests: A Guide to the Advanced Placement Program*. Princeton, N.J.: Educational Testing Service, 1979.

Commission on the Reorganization of Secondary Education. *Cardinal Principles of Secondary Education*. Bulletin 35. Washington, D.C.: National Education Association, 1918.

Conlan, John B. "MACOS: The Push for a National Curriculum." *Social Education* 39 (October 1975): 388–392.

Connecticut Department of Education. *Guide to Curriculum Development in Social Studies*. Hartford, Conn.: State of Connecticut Board of Education, 1981.

Cooley, William W., and Leinhardt, Gaea. *The Instructional Dimensions Study: The Search for Effective Classroom Processes: Final Report*. Pittsburgh: Learning Research and Development Center, University of Pittsburgh, 1978.

Copperman, Paul. "The Achievement Decline of the 1970s." *Phi Delta Kappan* 60 (June 1979): 736–739.

Counts, George S. *Dare the Schools Build a New Social Order?* New York: John Day, 1932.

Curti, Merle. *The Social Ideas of American Educators*. Paterson, N.J.: Littlefield, Adams & Co., 1959.

Cusick, Philip A. *Inside High School: The Student's World*. New York: Holt, Rinehart and Winston, 1973.

Dallas Independent School District. *Social Studies Baseline*. Dallas, Tx., 1978.

Davis, James E., and Haley, Frances. *Planning a Social Studies Program*. Boulder, Colo.: Social Science Education Consortium, 1977.

Davis, O. L.; Frymier, Jack R.; and Clinefelter, David L. "Curriculum Materials Used by Eleven-Year-Old Pupils: An Analysis Using the Annehurst Curriculum Classification System." Paper presented at the annual meeting of the American Educational Research Association, New York, April 1977.

Declared Competencies Index. Baltimore: Maryland Department of Education, Project Basic, 1979.

Dewey, John. *How We Think*. Boston: D. C. Heath, 1910.

Dewey, John. *How We Think: A Restatement of the Relation of Reflective Thinking to the Educative Process*. Boston: D. C. Heath, 1933.

Diem, Richard A. *Computers in the Social Studies Classroom.* How-To-Do-It Series 2, No. 14. Washington, D.C.: National Council for the Social Studies, 1981.

Doll, Ronald C. *Curriculum Improvement.* 2nd ed. Boston: Allyn and Bacon, 1970.

Dow, Peter B. "MACOS Revisited: A Commentary on the Most Frequently Asked Questions About Man: A Course of Study." *Social Education* 39 (October 1975): 388–389, 393–396.

Dreeban, Robert. *The Nature of Schools and the Work of Teachers.* Glenview, Ill.: Scott Foresman, 1970.

Dufty, David. "Living Skills as a Core Curriculum Component." Sydney: University of Sydney, 1980.

Dufty, David. "Planning for Social Studies Instruction." In *UNESCO Handbook for the Teaching of Social Studies.* Edited by H. Mehlinger. Paris: UNESCO, 1981.

Dunn, Arthur William. *The Social Studies in Secondary Education.* Bulletin No. 28. Washington, D.C.: U.S. Department of the Interior, Bureau of Education, 1916.

Early Adolescence: Perspectives and Recommendations. Washington, D.C.: National Science Foundation, 1978.

Edgerton, Ronald B. "Odyssey of a Book: How a Social Studies Text Comes Into Being." *Social Education* 33 (March 1969): 279–286.

Egan, K. "The Student and the Secondary Social Studies Curriculum." *Theory and Research in Social Education* 6 (1978): 1–19.

Ehman, Lee H. "Research on Social Studies Curriculum and Instruction: Values." In *Review of Research on Social Studies Education: 1970–1975.* Boulder, Colo.: ERIC Clearinghouse for Social Studies/Social Science Education, and Social Science Education Consortium; Washington, D.C.: National Council for the Social Studies, 1977.

Ehman, Lee H. "Research in Social Studies Education: Implications for Teaching Citizenship." *Social Education* 43 (November/December 1979): 594–596.

Eisner, Elliot W. *The Educational Imagination: On the Design and Evaluation of School Programs.* New York: Macmillan, 1979.

Engle, Shirley H. "Decision Making: The Heart of Social Studies Instruction." *Social Education* 24 (November 1960): 301–304, 306.

EPIE. *Report on a National Study of the Nature and the Quality of Instructional Materials Most Used by Teachers and Learners.* EPIE Report No. 71. New York: Educational Products Information Exchange Institute, 1976.

EPIE. *Report on a National Study of the Nature and the Quality of Instructional Materials Most Used by Teachers and Learners.* EPIE Report No. 76. New York: Educational Products Information Exchange Institute, 1977.

"Essentials of Education, The." Pamphlet issued by the Organizations for the Essentials of Education, 1981.

"Essentials of the Social Studies." *Social Education* 45 (March 1981): 163–164.

Evaluative Criteria. Arlington, Va.: National Study of School Evaluation, 1978.

Fancett, Verna S. Personal conversation with Project SPAN staff, April 1979.

Fancett, Verna S., and Hawke, Sharryl. "Instructional Practices in Social Studies." In *The Current State of Social Studies: A Report of Project SPAN.* Boulder, Colo.: Social Science Education Consortium, 1982.

Farman, Greg; Natriello, Gary; and Dornbusch, Sanford M. "Social Studies and Motivation: High School Students' Perceptions of the Articulation of Social Studies to Work, Family, and Community." *Theory and Research in Social Education* 6 (September 1978): 27–39.

Fenton, Edwin. *Developing a New Curriculum: A Rationale for the Holt Social Studies Curriculum.* New York: Holt, Rinehart and Winston, 1967.

Fenton, Edwin. "The Implications of Lawrence Kohlberg's Research for Civic Education." In *Education for Responsible Citizenship.* Edited by B. F. Brown. New York: McGraw-Hill, 1977.

Fernandez, Celestino; Massey, Grace Carroll; and Dornbusch, Sanford M. *High School Students' Perceptions of Social Studies.* Occasional Paper No. 6. Stanford, Calif.: Stanford Center for Research and Development in Teaching, Stanford University, 1975.

Fetsko, William. "Textbooks and the New Social Studies." *Social Studies* 70 (March/April 1979): 51–55.

Fielding, Roger. "Social Education and Social Change: Constraints of the Hidden Curricula." In *Social/Political Education in Three Countries.* Edited by I. Morrissett and A. M. Williams. Boulder, Colo.: Social Science Education Consortium and ERIC Clearinghouse for Social Studies/Social Science Education, 1981.

Fisher, Charles W., and others. *Teaching Behaviors, Academic Learning Time and Student Achievement: Final Report of Phase III-B, Beginning Teacher Evaluation Study.* Sacramento: California State Commission for Teacher Preparation and Licensing, 1978.

FitzGerald, Frances. *America Revised: History Schoolbooks in the Twentieth Century.* Boston: Little Brown, 1979.

Flieger, Howard. "The Economics Gap." *U.S. News and World Report,* January 31, 1977.

Fontana, Lynn. *Perspectives on the Social Studies.* Research Report No. 78. Bloomington, Ind.: Agency for Instructional Television, 1980a.

Fontana, Lynn. *Status of Social Studies Teaching Practices in Secondary Schools.* Research Report No. 79. Bloomington, Ind.: Agency for Instructional Television, 1980b.

Foshay, Arthur W., and Burton, William W. "Citizenship as the Aim of Social Studies." *Theory and Research in Social Education* 4 (December 1976): 1–22.

Fox, Karen F. A., and others. "Graduation Competency Testing in the Social Studies: A Position Statement of the National Council for the Social Studies." *Social Education* 43 (May 1979).

Fraenkel, Jack R. "Goals for Teaching Values and Value Analysis." *Journal of Research and Development in Education* 13 (Winter 1980): 93–102.

Frazier, Alexander. "Open Letter to a Proposed Commission on the Social Studies." *Social Education* 26 (March 1962): 141–146.

Gallup, George H. "The Tenth Annual Gallup Poll of the Public's Attitudes Toward the Public Schools." *Phi Delta Kappan* 60 (September 1978): 33–45.

Gallup, George H. "The Eleventh Annual Gallup Poll of the Public's Attitudes Toward the Public Schools." *Phi Delta Kappan* 61 (September 1979): 33–46.

Ganz, Rochelle. "Social Studies Teachers as Political Participants." *Social Education* 45 (October 1981): 408–411.

Garcia, Jesus. "The American Indian: No Longer a Forgotten American in U.S. History Texts Published in the 1970s." *Social Education* 44 (February 1980): 148–152, 164.

Gil, David G. "The Hidden Success of Schooling in the United States." In *Educating America.* Edited by T. J. Hynes, Jr., D. W. Sutherland, and D. K. Sutherland. Skokie, Ill.: National Textbook Co., 1981.

Goldstein, Paul. *Changing the American School Book.* Lexington, Mass.: D. C. Heath, 1978.

Goldstein, Phyllis. Personal conversation with Project SPAN staff, October 1980.

Goodlad, John I., and Klein, M. Francis. *Behind the Classroom Door.* Worthington, Ohio: Charles A. Jones, 1970.

Gooler, Dennis. "Strategies for Obtaining Clarification of Priorities in Education." Doctoral dissertation, University of Illinois, Urbana, 1971. (Quoted in Stake and Easley, 1978.)

Grannis, Joseph C. "The Social Studies Teacher and Research on Teacher Education." *Social Education* 34 (March 1970): 291–301.

Grannis, Joseph C. "Classroom Culture and the Problem of Control." In *Considered Action for Curriculum Improvement.* Edited by A. W. Foshay. Alexandria, Va.: Association for Supervision and Curriculum Development, 1980.

Gross, Richard E. "The Status of the Social Studies in the Public Schools of the United States: Facts and Impressions From a National Survey." *Social Education* 41 (March 1977): 194–200, 205.

Guerriero, Carl A. "What are School Priorities? A Public Survey." *Educational Leadership* 37 (January 1980): 344–345.

Haas, John D. *The Era of the New Social Studies.* Boulder, Colo.: Social Science Education Consortium, Inc., and ERIC Clearinghouse for Social Studies/Social Science Education, 1977.
Haas, John D. "Social Studies: Where Have We Been? Where Are We Now?" *Social Studies* 70 (July/August 1979): 147–154.
Haas, John D. "Society, Social Justice, and Social/Political Education: A Reaction." In *Social/Political Education in Three Countries.* Edited by I. Morrissett and A. M. Williams, Boulder, Colo.: ERIC Clearinghouse for Social Studies/Social Science Education, and Social Science Education Consortium, 1980.
Haas, John D. "The Uses of Rationales, Goals and Objectives in the Social Studies." *Social Studies* 72 (November/December 1981): 249–253.
Haas, John D., and Van Scotter, Richard. "An Inquiry Model for the Social Studies." *NASSP Bulletin* (March 1974): 74–81.
Hagen, Owen A., and Stansberry, Steve T. "Why Inquiry?" *Social Education* 33 (May 1969): 534–537.
Hanna, Paul R. "Revising the Social Studies: What Is Needed?" *Social Education* 27 (April 1963): 190–196.
Hansen, W. Lee. "The State of Economic Literacy." In *Perspectives on Economic Education.* Edited by D. Wentworth, W. L. Hansen, and S. Hawke. Boulder, Colo.: Social Science Education Consortium, 1977.
Harrington, Charles. "Textbooks and Political Socialization: A Multivariate Analysis." *Teaching Political Science* 7 (1980): 481–499.
Hart, Leslie A. *How the Brain Works: A New Understanding of Human Learning, Emotion, and Thinking.* New York: Basic Books, 1975.
Havelock, Ronald G. *Planning for Innovation Through Dissemination and Utilization of Knowledge.* Ann Arbor, Mich.: Center for Research on Utilization of Scientific Knowledge, 1971.
Helburn, Nicholas, and Helburn, Suzanne Wiggins. "Stability and Reform in Recent American Curriculum." Unpublished paper, 1978.
Helburn, Suzanne W. "Comments." In *Defining the Social Studies.* Edited by R. D. Barr, J. L. Barth, and S. S. Shermis. Arlington, Va.: National Council for the Social Studies, 1977.
Hefley, James C. *Textbooks on Trial.* Wheaton, Ill.: Victor Books, 1976.
"Help! Teacher Can't Teach!" *Time,* June 16, 1980, pp. 54–63.
Henning, Joel F., and others. *Mandate for Change: The Impact of Law on Educational Innovation.* Chicago: American Bar Association; Boulder, Colo.: Social Science Education Consortium; Eugene, Ore.: ERIC Clearinghouse on Educational Management, 1979.
Hertzberg, Hazel W. *Social Studies Reform: 1880–1980.* Report of Project SPAN. Boulder, Colo.: Social Science Education Consortium, 1981.
Herz, Martin F. "How the Cold War is Taught." *Social Education* 43 (February 1979): 118–122.
High School Graduation Requirements. Atlanta, Ga.: Georgia State Board of Education, 1976.
Historical Statistics of the United States, Colonial Times to 1970: Parts 1 and 2. Washington, D.C.: Bureau of the Census, U.S. Department of Commerce, 1975.
Holman, Evelyn Lezzer. "The School Ecosystem." In *Considered Action for Curriculum Improvement.* Edited by A. W. Foshay. Alexandria, Va.: Association for Supervision and Curriculum Development, 1980.
Hornbeck, David W. "Maryland's Project Basic." *Educational Leadership* 35 (November 1977): 98–101.
Hughes, Andrew S. "Separate Subject and Integrated Approaches to Social Education." *History and Social Science Teacher* 13 (Spring 1978) 163–167.

Hunt, Maurice P., and Metcalf, Lawrence E. *Teaching High School Social Studies.* New York: Harper and Row, 1955.

Hunt, Maurice P., and Metcalf, Lawrence E. *Teaching High School Social Studies.* 2nd ed. New York: Harper and Row, 1968.

Hunter, Madeline. "Teaching is Decision Making." *Educational Leadership* 37 (October 1979): 62–67.

Husek, T. R., and Sirotnik, Ken. "Matrix Sampling." *Evaluation Comment* (December 1968).

Hyman, Herbert; Wright, Charles; and Reed, John Shelton. *The Enduring Effects of Education.* Chicago: University of Chicago Press, 1975.

Jackson, Philip W. *Life in Classrooms.* New York: Holt, Rinehart and Winston, 1968.

Jantzen, Steven L. "What Textbooks Will Be Like in 1985." *Media and Methods* 15 (January 1979): 70–72.

Jarolimek, John. "The Social Studies: An Overview." In *The Social Studies: Eightieth Yearbook of the National Council for the Study of Education, Part 2.* Chicago: University of Chicago Press, 1981.

Jencks, Christopher, and others. *Inequality: A Reassessment of the Effect of Family and Schooling in America.* New York: Basic Books, 1972.

Johnson, Roger E. "Teachers Beware: Elementary Social Studies Textbooks are Getting Harder to Read." Paper presented at the annual meeting of the National Council for the Social Studies, Atlanta, November 26–29, 1975.

Joyce, Bruce R. *New Strategies for Social Education.* Chicago: Science Research Associates, 1972.

Joyce, William W., and Alleman-Brooks, Janet E. *Teaching Social Studies in the Elementary and Middle Schools.* New York: Holt, Rinehart and Winston, 1979.

Joyce, William W., and Alleman-Brooks, Janet. "Resolving the Identity Crisis in Elementary and Middle School Social Studies." *Journal of Research and Development in Education* 13 (Winter 1980): 60–71.

Kane, Michael B. *Minorities in Textbooks: A Study of Their Treatment in Social Studies Texts.* Chicago: Quadrangle Books, 1970.

Kitchens, James A., and Muessig, Raymond H. *The Study and Teaching of Sociology.* Columbus, Ohio: Charles E. Merrill, 1980.

Klein, M. Frances; Tye, Kenneth A.; and Wright, Joyce E. "A Study of Schooling: Curriculum." *Phi Delta Kappan* 61 (December 1979): 224–248.

Kohlberg, Lawrence. "The Cognitive-Developmental Approach to Moral Education." *Phi Delta Kappan* 56 (June 1975): 670–677.

Komoski, P. Kenneth. "The Realities of Choosing and Using Instructional Materials." *Educational Leadership* 36 (October 1978): 46–49.

Krathwohl, David R.; Bloom, Benjamin S.; and Masia, Bertram B. *Taxonomy of Educational Objectives: The Classification of Educational Goals. Handbook II: The Affective Domain.* New York: David McKay, 1964.

Kuhn, Alfred. *The Logic of Social Systems.* San Francisco: Jossey-Bass, 1974.

Kuhn, Alfred. *Unified Social Science: A System-Based Introduction.* Homewood, Ill.: Dorsey Press, 1975.

Kurfman, Dana G., ed. *Developing Decision-Making Skills.* Arlington, Va.: National Council for the Social Studies, 1977.

Kurfman, Dana G. "Evaluation in Social Studies." In *Working Papers from Project SPAN.* A Project SPAN report. Boulder, Colo.: Social Science Education Consortium, 1982.

Lawton, Denis. "Foundations for the Social Studies." In *UNESCO Handbook for the Teaching of Social Studies.* Edited by H. Mehlinger. Paris: UNESCO, 1981.

Leming, James E. "Research in Social Studies Education: Implications for Teaching Values." *Social Education* 43 (November/December 1979): 597–598, 601.

Lengel, James G. "Concepts and Skills: Social Studies in 2002." In *Working Papers from Project SPAN*. Boulder, Colo.: Social Science Education Consortium, 1982.

Lengel, James G., and Superka, Douglas P. "Curriculum Organization in Social Studies." In *The Current State of Social Studies: A Report of Project SPAN*. Boulder, Colo.: Social Science Education Consortium, 1982.

Lockwood, Alan L. "The Effects of Values Clarification and Moral Development Curricula on School Age Subjects: A Critical Review of Recent Research." *Review of Educational Research* 48 (Summer 1978): 325–364.

Lortie, Dan. "The Balance of Control and Autonomy in Elementary School Teaching." In *The Semi-Professions and Their Organization*. Edited by A. Etzioni. New York: Free Press, 1969.

Lortie, Dan C. *Schoolteacher: A Sociological Study*. Chicago: University of Chicago Press, 1975.

Lunstrum, John P. "Reading in the Social Studies: A Preliminary Analysis of Recent Research." *Social Education* 41 (January 1976): 10–18.

Main, Robert S. "The Treatment of Economic Issues in High School Government, Sociology, U.S. History and World History Texts." *Journal of Economic Education* 9 (September 1978): 115–118.

Marker, Gerald W. "Goals for Political and Social Participation." *Journal of Research and Development in Education* 31 (Winter 1980a): 72–81.

Marker, Gerald W. "Why Schools Abandon 'New Social Studies' Materials." *Theory and Research in Social Education* 7 (Winter 1980b): 35–57.

Martin, John Henry. "Reconsidering the Goals of High School Education." *Educational Leadership* 37 (January 1980): 278–285.

Martorella, Peter H. "Research on Social Studies Learning and Instruction: Cognition." In *Review of Research in Social Studies Education: 1970–1975*. Boulder, Colo.: Social Science Education Consortium and ERIC Clearinghouse for Social Studies/Social Science Education; Washington, D.C.: National Council for the Social Studies, 1977.

Martorella, Peter H. "Cognition Research: Some Implications for the Design of Social Studies Instructional Materials." Paper presented at the annual meeting of the American Educational Research Association, San Francisco, April 10, 1979a.

Martorella, Peter H. "Part II, Research in Social Studies Education: Implications for Teaching in the Cognitive Domain." *Social Education* 43 (November/December 1979b): 599–601.

Martorella, Peter H. "Social Studies Goals in the Middle Grades." *Journal of Research and Development in Education* 13 (Winter 1980): 47–59.

McLaughlin, Milbrey Wallin, and Marsh, David D. "Staff Development and School Change." *Teacher's College Record* 80 (September 1978): 69–94.

McPherson, Gertrude. *Small Town Teacher*. Cambridge, Mass.: Harvard University Press, 1972.

Mehlinger, Howard D. "Foreword." In *Defining the Social Studies*. Edited by R. D. Barr, J. L. Barth, and S. S. Shermis. Arlington, Va.: National Council for the Social Studies, 1977.

Mehlinger, Howard. "Social Studies: Some Gulfs and Priorities." In *The Social Studies: Eightieth Yearbook of the National Society for the Study of Education*. Chicago: University of Chicago Press, 1981.

Mendlovitz, Saul H.; Metcalf, Lawrence; and Washburn, Michael. "The Crisis of Global Transformation, Interdependence, and the Schools." In *Education for Responsible Citizenship*. Edited by B. F. Brown. New York: McGraw-Hill, 1977.

Metcalf, Lawrence E., ed. *Values Education: Rationale, Strategies, and Procedures*. Washington, D.C.: National Council for the Social Studies, 1971.

Meyer, LeAnn. *The Citizenship Education Issue: Problems and Programs*. Denver: Education Commission of the States, 1979.

Michaelis, John U. *Social Studies for Children in a Democracy*. Englewood Cliffs, N.J.: Prentice-Hall, 1976.

Michaelis, John U. "Basic Features of Social Studies/Social Science Education." *Social Studies Review* 18 (Winter 1979): 35–41.

Michaelis, John U. *Social Studies for Children: A Guide to Basic Instruction.* Englewood Cliffs, N.J.: Prentice-Hall, 1980.

Michigan Department of Education. "A Rationale for Social Studies Education in Michigan." (Draft.) Lansing: Michigan Department of Education, 1980.

Miller, Warren E., and others. *American National Election Studies Data Sourcebook 1952–1978.* Ann Arbor, Mich.: University of Michigan Center for Political Studies, 1980.

Millman, Jason. "Criterion-Referenced Measurement." In *Evaluation in Education.* Edited by W. J. Popham. Berkeley, Calif.: McCutchan, 1974.

Mitsakos, Charles L. "A Global Education Program Can Make a Difference." *Theory and Research in Social Education* 6 (March 1978): 1–15.

Moore, Jerry R. "Social Studies Assessment: Current Practice." In *Criterion-Referenced Testing in Social Studies.* Edited by P. L. Williams and J. R. Moore. Washington, D.C.: National Council for the Social Studies, 1980.

Morrissett, Irving. "Curriculum Information Network. Sixth Report: Preferred Approaches to the Teaching of Social Studies." *Social Education* 41 (March 1977): 206–209.

Morrissett, Irving. "Citizenship, Social Studies, and the Academician." *Social Education* 43 (January 1979): 12–17.

Morrissett, Irving. "Citizenship, Socialization, and History." Paper presented at the annual conference of the Social Science Education Consortium, Guildford, England, July 1980.

Morrissett, Irving. "The Needs of the Future and the Constraints of the Past." In *Social Studies: Eightieth Yearbook of the National Society for the Study of Education, Part 2.* Edited by H. D. Mehlinger and O. L. Davis, Jr. Chicago: University of Chicago Press, 1981a.

Morrissett, Irving. "Romance and Realism in Citizenship Education." *Social Studies* 72 (January/February 1981b): 15–17.

Morrissett, Irving, and Stevens, W. Williams, Jr., eds. *Social Science in the Schools: A Search for Rationale.* New York: Holt, Rinehart and Winston, 1971.

Morrissett, Irving, and Haas, John D. "Rationale, Goals, and Objectives in Social Studies." In *The Current State of Social Studies: A Report of Project SPAN.* Boulder, Colo.: Social Science Education Consortium, 1982.

Mullis, Ina V. S. "Review of Sequential Tests of Education Progress: Social Studies." In *The Eighth Mental Measurements Yearbook.* Edited by O. K. Buros. Highland Park, N.J.: Gryphon Press, 1978.

Mullis, Ina V. S. *Effects of Home and School on Learning Mathematics, Political Knowledge, and Political Attitudes.* Denver: National Assessment of Educational Progress, 1979.

Myrdal, Gunnar. *An American Dilemma.* New York: Harper and Bros., 1944.

NAEP. *Social Studies Objectives.* Denver: National Assessment of Educational Progress, 1970.

NAEP. *Citizenship Objectives for 1974–75 Assessment.* Denver: National Assessment of Educational Progress, 1972.

NAEP. "Lay and Subject Matter Reviews of National Assessment Basic Skills Objectives, June 18 to June 25, 1975." Unpublished paper. Denver: National Assessment of Educational Progress, 1975.

NAEP. *Education for Citizenship: A Bicentennial Survey.* Denver: National Assessment of Educational Progress, 1976.

NAEP. *Changes in Political Knowledge and Attitudes, 1969–76.* Denver, National Assessment of Educational Progress, 1978a.

NAEP. *Changes in Social Studies Performance, 1972–76.* Denver: National Assessment of Educational Progress, 1978b.

NAEP. *NAEP Newsletter.* Denver: National Assessment of Educational Progress, August 1979.

NAEP. *Citizenship and Social Studies Objectives: 1981–82 Assessment.* Denver: National Assessment of Educational Progress, 1980.

National Commission on the Reform of Secondary Education. *The Reform of Secondary Education.* New York: McGraw-Hill, 1973.

National Council for the Social Studies. "Social Studies and Its Career Implications." In *Career Education in the Academic Classroom.* Edited by G. L. Mangum and others. Salt Lake City: Olympus, 1975.

National Research Council. *The State of School Science.* Washington, D.C.: Commission on Human Resources, 1979.

National Task Force for High School Reform. *The Adolescent, Other Citizens, and Their High Schools.* New York: McGraw-Hill, 1975.

Nelson, Jack L., and Palonsky, Stuart. "Preservice Teacher Perceptions of Social Education." Paper presented at the American Educational Research Association Conference, San Francisco, 1979.

Nelson, Jack L., and Michaelis, John U. *Secondary Social Studies Instruction, Curriculum, Evaluation.* Englewood Cliffs, N.J.: Prentice-Hall, 1980.

Nelson, Lynn R. "Social Studies Teachers: Their Views of Their Profession." *Social Education* 45 (October 1981): 418–420.

Newmann, Fred M. *Education for Citizen Action: Challenge for Secondary Curriculum.* Berkeley: McCutchan, 1975.

Newmann, Fred M. "Building a Rationale for Civic Education." In *Building Rationales for Citizenship Education.* Edited by J. P. Shaver. Arlington, Va.: National Council for the Social Studies, 1977.

Newmann, Fred M. "Political Participation: An Analytic Review and Proposal." In *Political Education in Flux.* Edited by J. Gillespie and D. Heater. London: Sage, 1980.

Newmann, Fred M., and Oliver, Donald W. *Clarifying Public Controversy: An Approach to Teaching Social Studies.* Boston: Little, Brown, 1970.

Newmann, Fred M.; Bertocci, Thomas A.; and Landsness, Ruthanne M. *Skills in Citizen Action: An English-Social Studies Program for Secondary Schools.* Madison, Wisc.: Citizen Participation Curriculum Project, 1977.

Ochoa, Anna S. "A Profile of Social Studies Teachers." *Social Education* 45 (October 1981): 401–404.

Oliver, Donald W., and Shaver, James P. *Teaching Public Issues in the High School.* Boston: Houghton Mifflin, 1966.

Oliver, Donald W., and Newmann, Fred M. *The Public Issues Series.* Cambridge, Mass.: Harvard University Press, 1967–1972.

Panel on Youth, President's Science Advisory Committee. *Youth: Transition to Adulthood.* Chicago: University of Chicago Press, 1974.

Parlee, Mary Brown. "The Friendship Bond: PT's Survey Report on Friendship in America." *Psychology Today* 13 (October 1979): 43–54.

Patrick, John J. "Political Socialization and Political Education in Schools." In *Handbook of Political Socialization.* Edited by S. A. Renshon. New York: Macmillan, 1977.

Patrick, John J. "Junior High School Students' Learning in Social Studies." In *Working Papers from Project SPAN.* Boulder, Colo.: Social Science Education Consortium, 1982.

Patrick, John J., with Hawke, Sharryl. "Social Studies Curriculum Materials." In *The Current State of Social Studies: A Report of Project SPAN.* Boulder, Colo.: Social Science Education Consortium, 1982.

Pearson, Floyd H. "A Content Analysis of the Treatment of Black People and Race Relations in United States History Textbooks." Doctoral dissertation, University of Minnesota, 1976.

Ponder, Gerald. "The More Things Change . . .: The Status of the Social Studies." *Educational Leadership* 36 (April 1979): 515–518.

Popham, W. James. "Well-Crafted Criterion-Referenced Tests." *Educational Leadership* 36 (November 1978): 91–95.
Pratt, David. *Curriculum: Design and Development.* New York: Harcourt Brace Jovanovich, 1980.

Rappaport, Sandra Joyce. "Teacher-Student Questioning and Approval/Disapproval Behavior in High School Social Studies." Summarized in *Social Studies Dissertations: 1973–1976.* Edited by P. R. Wrubel and R. Ratliff. Boulder, Colo.: ERIC Clearinghouse for Social Studies/Social Science Education, and Social Science Education Consortium, 1978.
Rasmussen, Robert T. "The Marketing of Educational Materials in America." Paper prepared for the international conference of PIRA, September 1978.
Raths, Louis E.; Harmin, Merrill; and Simon, Sidney B. *Values and Teaching.* 2nd ed. Columbus, Ohio: Charles E. Merrill, 1978.
Remy, Richard C. "Making, Judging, and Influencing Decisions: A Focus for Citizen Education." *Social Education* 40 (October 1976): 360–365.
Remy, Richard C. *Consumer and Citizenship Education Today: A Comparative Analysis of Key Assumptions.* Columbus, Ohio: Mershon Center, Ohio State University, 1978a.
Remy, Richard C. "Social Studies and Citizenship Education: Elements of a Changing Relationship." *Theory and Research in Social Education* 6 (December 1978b): 40–59.
Remy, Richard C. *Citizenship and Consumer Education: Key Assumptions and Basic Competencies.* Bloomington, Ind.: Phi Delta Kappa Educational Foundation, 1980.
Remy, Richard C., and Anderson, Lee. "Political Education in the Public Schools: The Challenge for Political Science." Report of the American Political Science Association Committee on Pre-Collegiate Education, 1971.
"Revision of the NCSS Social Studies Curriculum Guidelines." *Social Education* 43 (April 1979): 261–278.
Rinehart, Sue T. "The Mischief of Factions: Political Parties in School Textbooks." Paper presented at the annual meeting of the American Political Science Association, Washington, D.C., August 31–September 3, 1979.
Risinger, C. Frederick. "Social Studies Teachers: A Personal Profile." *Social Education* 45 (October 1981): 405–407.
"Role of the Social Studies, The." *Social Education* 26 (October 1962): 315–318, 327.
Rose, Caroline B. *Sociology: The Study of Man in Society.* Columbus, Ohio: Charles E. Merrill, 1965.
Roselle, Daniel. "Editorial Reflections." *Social Education* 44 (January 1980): 6–9.
Rosenbaum, James E. *Making Inequality: The Hidden Curriculum of High School Tracking.* New York: John Wiley and Sons, 1976.
Rosenberg, Max. "Education for Pluralism." *Educational Leadership* 6 (October 1978): 70–71.
Rosenshine, Barak, and Furst, Norma. "Research on Teacher Performance Criteria." In *Research in Teacher Education: A Symposium.* Edited by B. O. Smith. Englewood Cliffs, N.J.: Prentice-Hall, 1971.
Rowe, Mary Budd. *Teaching Science as Continuous Inquiry: A Basic.* New York: McGraw-Hill, 1978.

Sarason, Seymour B. *The Culture of the School and the Problem of Change.* Boston: Allyn and Bacon, 1971.
Sargent, Linda, and Satterfield, Jane. *The Greenville County School District's Social Studies Curriculum.* Greenville, S.C.: Greenville County Schools, 1978.
Sax, Gilbert. "The Use of Standardized Tests in Evaluation." In *Evaluation in Education.* Edited by W. J. Popham. Berkeley: McCutchan, 1974.
Schneider, Donald O. "Tradition and Change in the Social Studies Curriculum." *Journal of Research and Development in Education* (Winter 1980): 12–23.

Schneider, Donald O., and Van Sickle, Ronald L. "The Status of the Social Studies: The Publishers' Perspective." *Social Education* 43 (October 1979): 461–465.

Scrupski, Adam. "The Social System of the School." In *Social Forces and Schooling.* Edited by N. K. Shimarara and A. Scrupski. New York: David McKay, 1975.

Selman, Robert L., and Selman, Anne P. "Children's Ideas About Friendship: A New Theory." *Psychology Today* 13 (October 1979): 71–80, 114.

Senesh, Lawrence. "Organizing a Curriculum Around Social Science Concepts." In *Concepts and Structure in the New Social Science Curricula.* Edited by I. Morrissett. New York: Holt, Rinehart and Winston, 1967.

Serow, Robert C., and Stike, Kenneth A. "Student Attitudes Toward High School Governance: Implications for Social Education." *Theory and Research in Social Education* 3 (September 1978): 14–26.

"Sex Rated Below Friends, School, and Sports." *Denver Post,* October 2, 1979.

Shaffarzick, J., and Sykes, C. "A Changing NIE: New Leadership, a New Climate." *Educational Leadership* 35 (February 1978): 367–372.

Shaver, James P. "Social Studies: The Need for Redefinition." *Social Education* 31 (November 1967): 588–592, 596.

Shaver, James P. "Comments of James P. Shaver." In *Defining the Social Studies.* Edited by R. D. Barr, J. L. Barth, and S. S. Shermis. Arlington, Va.: National Council for the Social Studies, 1977a.

Shaver, James P. "A Critical View of the Social Studies Profession." *Social Education* 41 (1977b): 300–307.

Shaver, James P. "The Task of Rationale-Building for Citizenship Education." In *Building Rationales for Citizenship Education.* Edited by J. P. Shaver. Arlington, Va.: National Council for the Social Studies, 1977c.

Shaver, James P. "The Usefulness of Educational Research in Curricular/Instructional Decision Making in Social Studies." *Theory and Research in Social Education* 7 (Fall 1979): 21–46.

Shaver, James P.; Davis, O. L.; and Helburn, Suzanne W. *An Interpretive Report on the Status of Pre-Collegiate Social Studies Education Based on Three NSF-Funded Studies.* Washington, D.C.: National Science Foundation, 1979a.

Shaver, James P.; Davis, O. L.; and Helburn, Suzanne W. "The Status of Social Studies Education: Impressions from Three NSF Studies." *Social Education* 43 February 1979b): 150–153.

Sikorski, Linda, and others. *Factors Influencing School Change.* San Francisco: Far West Laboratory for Educational Research and Development, 1976.

Silberman, Charles E. *Crisis in the Classroom: The Remaking of American Education.* New York: Random House, 1970.

Smith, David W. "Assessing the Impact of the 'New Social Studies' Upon School Curriculum: A Case Study of High School Sociology." Doctoral dissertation, Northwestern University, 1979.

Smith, Frederick R., and Patrick, John J. "Civics: Relating Social Study to Social Reality." In *Social Studies in the United States.* New York: Harcourt, Brace and World, 1967.

Social Studies for North Dakota Schools. Bismarck: North Dakota Department of Public Instruction, no date.

Soley, Mary. "Controversial Issues as Viewed by Social Studies Teachers." *Social Education* 45 (October 1981): 412–417.

Stake, Robert E., and Easley, Jack A., Jr. *Case Studies in Science Education.* Washington, D.C.: National Science Foundation, 1978.

Stanley, William B. "Toward a Reconstruction of Social Education." *Theory and Research in Social Education* 9 (Spring 1981): 67–89.

Starritt, David. *Social Studies Curriculum Guide.* Colorado Springs: Harrison School District 2, no date.

Statistical Abstract of the United States: 1980. 99th ed. Washington, D.C.: Bureau of the Census, U.S. Department of Commerce, 1980.

Stratemeyer, Florence B., and others. *Developing a Curriculum for Modern Living.* New York: Teachers College Press, 1947.

"Study Finds Schools Waste Pupils' Time." *The Denver Post*, October 11, 1981, p. 20A.

Stufflebeam, Daniel I., and others. *Educational Evaluation and Decision Making*. Itasca, Ill.: F. E. Peacock, 1971.

Superka, Douglas P., and others. *Values Education Sourcebook: Conceptual Approaches, Materials Analyses, and an Annotated Bibliography*. Boulder, Colo.: Social Science Education Consortium and ERIC Clearinghouse for Social Studies/Social Science Education, 1976.

Superka, Douglas P. *An Exploration of Social Studies Innovation in Secondary Schools*. Boulder, Colo.: Social Science Education Consortium, 1977.

Superka, Douglas P., and others. *Social Studies Evaluation Sourcebook*. Boulder, Colo., Social Science Education Consortium, 1978.

Superka, Douglas P.; Hawke, Sharryl; and Morrissett, Irving. "The Current and Future Status of Social Studies." *Social Education* 44 (May 1980): 362–369.

Sutton, Jerri. *National Survey in Social Studies Education, Kindergarten–Grade 12*. Richmond: Virginia Department of Education, 1976.

Taba, Hilda. *Curriculum Development*. New York: Harcourt, Brace and World, 1962.

Tanner, Daniel, and Tanner, Laurel N. *Curriculum Development: Theory Into Practice*. New York: Macmillan, 1975.

Taylor, Bob L., and others. *Tips for Infusing Career Education in the Curriculum*. Boulder, Colo.: Social Science Education Consortium, 1977.

TenBrink, Terry D. *Evaluation: A Practical Guide for Teachers*. New York: McGraw-Hill, 1974.

Torney, Judith V. "The Elementary School Years as an Optimal Period for Learning About International Human Rights." Paper presented at American Bar Association Symposium on Law and the Humanities: Implications for Elementary Education, Chicago, 1978.

Torney-Purta, Judith V. "Recent Psychological Research Relating to Children's Social Cognition and Its Implications for Social and Political Education." In *Social/Political Education in Three Countries*. Edited by I. Morrissett and A. M. Williams. Boulder, Colo.: ERIC Clearinghouse for Social Studies/Social Science Education, and Social Science Education Consortium, Inc., 1980.

Tri-County Goal Development Project. *Course Goals in Social Science, K–12*. Portland, Ore: Northwest Regional Educational Laboratory, 1976.

Tryon, Rollo M. *The Social Sciences as School Subjects*. New York: Charles Scribner's Sons, 1935.

Tucker, Jan L. "Research on Social Studies Teaching and Teacher Education." In *Review of Research in Social Studies Education: 1970–1975*. Boulder, Colo.: ERIC Clearinghouse for Social Studies/Social Science Education, and Social Science Education Consortium; Washington, D.C.: National Council for the Social Studies, 1977.

Turner, Mary Jane. *Developing Your Child's Citizenship Competence*. Boulder, Colo.: Social Science Education Consortium; Columbus, Ohio: Mershon Center, Ohio State University, 1980.

Turner, Mary Jane, and Haley, Frances. "Utilization of New Social Studies Curriculum Programs." In *Three Studies on Perception and Utilization of New Social Studies Materials*. Boulder, Colo.: Social Science Education Consortium, 1977.

Tyler, Ralph W. *Basic Principles of Curriculum and Instruction*. Chicago: University of Chicago Press, 1950.

Tyler, Ralph W. "The U.S. vs. the World: A Comparison of Educational Performance." *Phi Delta Kappan* 62 (January 1981): 307–310.

Van Scotter, Richard, and Haas, John D. "An Inquiry Model for the Social Studies." *NAASP Bulletin* 59 (March 1975): 74–81.

Vetter, Donald. "Summary Report: Decision-Making in Contemporary America." Unpublished paper, 1976.

Walberg, Herbert J.; Schiller, Diane; and Haertel, Geneva D. "The Quiet Revolution in Educational Research." *Phi Delta Kappan* 61 (November 1979): 179–183.

Walker, Constance. "Why Teachers Quit." *Pennsylvania School Journal* (May 1978): 144.

Waller, Willard W. *The Sociology of Teaching.* New York: Russell, 1961.

Wangen, Roger, ed. *Some Essential Learner Outcomes in Social Studies.* Minneapolis: Minnesota Department of Education, 1977.

Weiss, Iris R. *National Survey of Science, Mathematics, and Social Studies Education.* Washington, D.C.: National Science Foundation, 1978.

Welton, David A., and Mallan, John T. *Children and Their World: Teaching Elementary Social Studies.* Chicago: Rand McNally, 1976.

Wesley, Edgar B. *Teaching the Social Studies.* New York: D. C. Heath, 1937.

Wesley, Edgar B. "Foreword." In *The Nature of the Social Studies.* Edited by R. D. Barr, J. L. Barth, and S. S. Shermis. Palm Springs, Calif.: ETC Publications, 1978.

Wiley, Karen B. *The Status of Pre-College Science, Mathematics, and Social Science Education: 1955–1975.* Vol. 3. Washington, D.C.: National Science Foundation, 1977.

Williams, Paul L., and Moore, Jerry R., eds. *Criterion-Referenced Testing in Social Studies.* Washington, D.C.: National Council for the Social Studies, 1980.

Wirt, Frederick M., and Kirst, Michael W. "Curriculum Decisions in the Political System." In *The Political Web of American Schools.* Boston: Little, Brown, 1972.

Wisconsin Department of Public Instruction. *Program Improvement for Social Studies Education in Wisconsin.* Madison, Wisc.: Wisconsin Department of Public Instruction, 1977.

Wright, David P. "Social Studies in 38 Schools: Research Findings From a Study of Schooling." Paper presented at the annual meeting of the National Council for the Social Studies, Portland, Oregon, 1979.

Wright, David P. Correspondence with Project SPAN staff, May/June, 1980.

About the Authors

Mary Vann Eslinger is Coordinator for Economic Education, South Central Education Center, North Carolina State Department of Public Instruction, Raleigh.

Verna S. Fancett is consultant, textbook author, and retired social studies teacher and department chair, Jamesville-DeWitt High School, DeWitt, New York.

John D. Haas is Professor of Education, University of Colorado, Boulder.

Sharryl Davis Hawke is Director of Editorial for Graphic Learning Corporation, Boulder, Colorado.

Hazel Whitman Hertzberg is Professor of History and Education, Teachers College, Columbia University, New York City.

James G. Lengel is Division Director, Vermont State Department of Education, Montpelier.

Irving Morrissett is Professor of Economics, University of Colorado, and Executive Director, Social Science Education Consortium, Boulder, Colorado.

John J. Patrick is Professor of Education, Indiana University, Bloomington.

Douglas P. Superka is Senior Training Specialist, Corporate Training and Development, Storage Technology Corporation, Louisville, Colorado.

ASCD Publications, Fall 1982

Yearbooks

A New Look at Progressive Education
(610-17812) $8.00
Considered Action for Curriculum Improvement
(610-80186) $9.75
Education for an Open Society
(610-74012) $8.00
Feeling, Valuing, and the Art of Growing:
Insights into the Affective
(610-77104) $9.75
Improving the Human Condition
(610-78132) $9.75
Life Skills in School and Society
(610-17786) $5.50
Lifelong Learning—A Human Agenda
(610-79160) $9.75
Perceiving, Behaving, Becoming: A New Focus
for Education (610-17278) $5.00
Perspectives on Curriculum Development
1776-1976 (610-76078) $9.50
Schools in Search of Meaning
(610-75044) $8.50
Staff Development/Organization Development
(610-81232) $9.75
Supervision of Teaching (610-82262) $10.00

Books and Booklets

About Learning Materials (611-78134) $4.50
Adventuring, Mastering, Associating: New
Strategies for Teaching Children
(611-76080) $5.00
Applied Strategies for Curriculum Evaluation
(611-81240) $5.75
Approaches to Individualized Education
(611-80204) $4.75
Bilingual Education for Latinos
(611-78142) $6.75
Classroom-Relevant Research in the Language
Arts (611-78140) $7.50
Clinical Supervision—A State of the Art Review
(611-80194) $3.75
Curriculum Leaders: Improving Their Influence
(611-76084) $4.00
Curriculum Materials 1981 (611-81266) $3.00
Curriculum Materials 1982 (611-82268) $4.00
Curriculum Theory (611-77112) $7.00
Degrading the Grading Myths: A Primer of
Alternatives to Grades and Marks
(611-76082) $6.00
Developing Basic Skills Programs in
Secondary Schools (611-82264) $5.00
Developmental Supervision: Alternative
Practices for Helping Teachers Improve
Instruction (611-81234) $5.00
Educating English-Speaking Hispanics
(611-80202) $6.50
Educators' Challenge: Healthy Mothers,
Healthy Babies (611-81244) $4.00
Educators' Challenge Progressive Chart
(611-81252) $2.00
Effective Instruction (611-80212) $6.50
Elementary School Mathematics: A Guide to
Current Research (611-75056) $5.00
Eliminating Ethnic Bias in Instructional
Materials: Comment and Bibliography
(611-74020) $3.25
Global Studies: Problems and Promises for
Elementary Teachers (611-76086) $4.50
Handbook of Basic Citizenship Competencies
(611-80196) $4.75
Helping Teachers Manage Classrooms (611-
82266) $8.50

Humanistic Education: Objectives and
Assessment (611-78136) $4.75
Mathematics Education Research
(611-81238) $6.75
Measuring and Attaining the Goals of Education
(611-80210) $6.50
Middle School in the Making
(611-74024) $5.00
The Middle School We Need
(611-75060) $2.50
Moving Toward Self-Directed Learning
(611-79166) $4.75
Multicultural Education: Commitments, Issues,
and Applications (611-77108) $7.00
Needs Assessment: A Focus for Curriculum
Development (611-75048) $4.00
Open Education: Critique and Assessment
(611-75054) $4.75
Partners: Parents and Schools
(611-79168) $4.75
Professional Supervision for Professional
Teachers (611-75046) $4.50
Reschooling Society: A Conceptual Model
(611-17950) $2.00
The School of the Future—NOW
(611-17920) $3.75
Schools Become Accountable: A PACT
Approach (611-74016) $3.50
The School's Role as Moral Authority
(611-77110) $4.50
Selecting Learning Experiences: Linking
Theory and Practice (611-78138) $4.75
Social Studies for the Evolving Individual
(611-17952) $3.00
Social Studies in the 1980s
(611-82270) $8.75
Staff Development: Staff Liberation
(611-77106) $6.50
Supervision: Emerging Profession
(611-17796) $5.00
Supervision in a New Key (611-17926) $2.50
Urban Education: The City as a Living
Curriculum (611-80206) $6.50
Vitalizing the High School (611-74026) $3.50
Developmental Characteristics of Children and
Youth (wall chart) (611-75058) $2.00

Discounts on quantity orders of same title to
single address: 10-49 copies, 10%; 50 or more
copies, 15%. Make checks or money orders
payable to ASCD. Orders totaling $20.00 or
less must be prepaid. Orders from institutions
and businesses must be on official purchase
order form. Shipping and handling charges will
be added to billed purchase orders. *Please be
sure to list the stock number of each publication, shown in parentheses.*

Subscription to *Educational Leadership*—$18.00
a year. ASCD Membership dues: Regular (subscription [$18] and yearbook)—$38.00 a year;
Comprehensive (includes subscription [$18]
and yearbook plus other books and booklets
distributed during period of membership)—
$48.00 a year.

Order from:

**Association for Supervision and
Curriculum Development
225 North Washington Street
Alexandria, Virginia 22314**